Making Her Point Loud and Clear
The Story of a Warrior Mom on a Mission

Jeanine Gleba as told to
Paul Lavenhar

Cover photo by Tim Larsen Office of the Governor
Back photos courtesy of Gleba family and Office of the
Governor Photographer Tim Larsen

*"Maybe everything we've ever done
has been for love."* - Byron Katie

For Bill, Shain, Luke and Grace...my everything.

JOY AND FEAR

When you are expecting a baby, your heart is caught somewhere between pure joy and fear. Joy – we can't wait to find out who this person we created will be. Fear – we wonder if everything will turn out alright for our child. Every parent knows the anticipation – the tension between fear and joy - is unnerving. But, if your fear is realized, the hardest part for parents is to work past their despair and take action.

Jeanine and Bill Gleba were expecting their third child. A happily married couple who lived in the suburbs of northwest New Jersey, they had two sons – five-year-old Shain and one-year-old Luke. Jeanine worked from home as a systems analyst for a large telecommunications company, a position she had held since her college internship.

When Jeanine became pregnant with her third child, she had a routine AFP (alpha-fetoprotein) blood test. She had the test with both boys, and they both came back "normal." She was taken aback when her doctor called to tell her that this time the blood test was abnormal. He recommended an amniocentesis, and immediately Jeanine's mind was filled with a million questions – most importantly, what does this mean?

Jeanine was unnerved by the sight of the extremely long needle they were going to insert into her womb on December 23, 1998. The procedure took seconds, and afterwards Jeanine let out a sigh of relief. With Christmas and two young boys eagerly awaiting Santa, she was able to take her mind off of waiting for the test results.

A few days later Jeanine received the news over the phone. "The female karyotype reveals Trisomy 20 mosaicism." Her first reaction was "A girl!" Then with shaking hands she struggled to scribble down notes as she thought, "What the hell is Trisomy 20?"

After a few seconds Jeanine was in such shock and confusion that her brain couldn't even comprehend what was being said. Fortunately, the woman on the phone kept it short and recommended that Jeanine see a genetic counselor as quickly as possible given that she was 16 weeks along in her pregnancy.

"It didn't matter to me how far along I was as I would never terminate the pregnancy. However, I couldn't get there fast enough to find out what was wrong with my baby girl," Jeanine said.

The genetic counselor couldn't tell Bill and Jeanine much about Trisomy 20. They learned that T20M is a rare chromosome abnormality in which some cells are normal, but others are abnormal.

There have been very few cases of T20M and as a result few medical studies have been done. Bill and Jeanine did learn that in prenatally detected T20M the outcome for 90-95% of the cases is a healthy baby. The abnormal cases found unexplained fetal death or multiple congenital disorders including kidney problems, heart defects, facial dysmorphisms such as a cleft lip and deformed ears, and possible psychomotor delays that can impede the ability of brain to coordinate the body.

They were relieved to learn that the odds of having any baby born with a birth defect were 3 percent due to a lack of other risk factors: Jeanine was under 35, not a smoker, and never did drugs.

Afterwards Jeanine spent many hours doing research on the Internet and even corresponded with a father in England whose child had the condition. She also contacted the few doctors at various universities in the United States who were knowledgeable on the subject and kind enough to answer her questions.

"In hindsight I'm not sure if this was the best thing to do because there was very little information in 1999 and the potential abnormalities were heartbreaking," Jeanine said. "However, I felt it better to be prepared than live in ignorant bliss."

From that point on Jeanine had bi-weekly ultrasounds to watch the growth and development of the baby and monitor any abnormalities of the kidneys and heart. An echocardiogram was also performed.

"Every hour drive to the hospital was filled with worry, but I left each visit optimistic, knowing that so far everything was fine".

Jeanine's mother would send her words of encouragement like "When that little baby grows up, she will be saying 'thank you' for bringing me into this world where I am loved, and where I can give so much love to many. Remember no one except God is born perfect, and who is to say what is perfect in God's eyes?"

Jeanine's pregnancy with her daughter was filled with waiting, worry, anxiety, and many prayers. To ease her mind, she enjoyed window-shopping for baby girl clothes and discovering that there was at least triple the selection of girls' clothes compared to boys'. She thought, "No wonder little girls grow up to be fashion divas and shopaholics. It begins in the womb!"

Other than that alarming test result it was a completely normal pregnancy. However, a specialized neonatal team was assigned to be present during labor and delivery. No one knew what to expect when the baby was born given the potential heart and kidney problems or even what she would look like given the possible facial deformities.

Despite their concerns, the day Grace was born to Jeanine and Bill Gleba was a day full of joy. They had a beautiful, healthy baby girl despite the prenatal genetic tests indicating she might have serious problems. The specialized neonatal team quickly whisked Grace away for more tests – and every single test came back normal. A sense of relief washed over Jeanine and Bill. The word "normal" never sounded so good.

When Jeanine gave birth to her and Bill's 7-pound 4-ounce baby girl, Jeanine felt, "She was an absolutely perfect baby girl. We named her Grace Isabelle, as she truly was a 'blessing from God.' My 'belle' was a beauty to behold. For a baby with many severe potential problems at birth it was sheer delight to hear her Apgar test scores to determine her health right after she was born were 9 and 10."

Jeanine and Bill were relieved that the test results meant they didn't need to worry anymore. They were prepared for the worst, and thrilled about having a healthy little girl. But, the next day their joy was followed by fear.

Grace had failed her newborn hearing-screening test. Deaf? How could that be? So many questions raced through their minds. How will she be able to interact with other kids? How will we communicate with her? Will she go to college? "Initially, we didn't focus on her failing a newborn hearing screening because we were so happy she was healthy," Jeanine remembers. "Based on the prenatal tests, all we could think about was whether she might have heart or kidney problems. When we were told she was deaf, it just didn't hit us at first. But when it sank in, we thought there's no history of deafness in our families, so how the hell can that be?"

Grace failed a second hearing test before she left the hospital. At first, Bill held out hope that the test results were wrong. "The doctors and nurses said, 'Well we don't really know. It's a screening, not a comprehensive hearing test.' When all her other tests for T20M came out normal, we hoped the hearings tests were false positives. But, we soon learned they weren't."

"The hospital audiologist called us up after the second test. She recommended that we should go to an ear, nose and throat (ENT) doctor to check again with more thorough testing. It was a real quick phone call. I sat down and cried before I called Bill."

More questions were seeping into Jeanine's mind. What exactly does this mean? In all the research on Grace's genetic issue "T20M" there was no mention of deafness. How could she be deaf? To Jeanine, it was absolutely mind-boggling. "We brought Grace home from the hospital. Not surprising in our own denial, we held out hope that it was just a fluke or a false positive test result. It didn't diminish our joy of bringing home our hearty and most definitely in the pink baby girl. We left the hospital with her big brothers in our two-door Honda Accord. I smile thinking of how we were able to fit an infant seat, car seat and booster seat in that small backseat."

In those first days after Grace's diagnosis Jeanine's head spun with unknowns and uncertainties. Can she hear anything? What kind of a life will she have? What kind of relationships will she have? Will she need to learn sign language? Will we? How will she succeed in school? Will she ever call me "Mom?"

Jeanine could not fathom a world of silence. "With every sound I heard, my sadness deepened. I thought of all the times I spoke to Grace when she was in my womb, and she hadn't heard a word. When I thought of all that silence, I could not stop my tears."

As their family and friends congratulated Jeanine and Bill on their beautiful baby girl, they struggled to find gentle ways to tell them: "She can't hear you."

For Bill, it was extremely upsetting and emotional. "It was tough because you must deal with the situation to begin with. But then, you need to explain it to everybody, so you have to keep reliving it every time or dealing with it every time that you tell the story over and over. Over time we became experts about Grace without the medical degrees."

It was definitely tough telling their parents, but even more difficult telling Grace's two older brothers - Shain and Luke.

Even though he was only six, Shain will never forget that day. "I vividly remember the day Mom told me. I was six, and she took me out for ice cream in Clinton. She sat with me on a bench, and she said the reason I took you out is to tell you that your sister has a hearing loss. She was very emotional. I didn't even really comprehend it, but she started crying, and I started crying, too. I didn't really fully comprehend it until Grace started to get older, and you did notice that like you would say something, and she didn't necessarily hear it. She didn't have her hearing aids when she was first born, so she wasn't able to listen. She didn't hear you."

Jeanine said, "I kind of knew from the get go there was no way that the majority of our extended family would learn sign language. At the time we didn't even know about the other options. So much happens in those first three months. It was a whirlwind. It was almost like when somebody dies. You are so caught up in planning the funeral, planning the wake, all that stuff - that it's not until few weeks later that you are able to really think and experience the sadness. It was kind of like that, too, when we found out about Grace's deafness. We were experiencing that sadness, but at the same time you are learning that you do have options and that there are different philosophies about how to handle it."

"We faced down the inevitable feelings of 'Why us?' I'd had a difficult pregnancy, so I'd realized there might be further problems. I never knew fear until I had my first child. Now I had a child who couldn't hear, and all those earlier fears intensified beyond comprehension. I felt as if I would always fear for her safety. I piled that onto my fears about communication and deteriorating prognoses."

Jeanine was not the type of person to sit back and do nothing when she was hit with bad news. "We are kind of action people," Jeanine said. A family friend, a speech therapist, who knew a great deal about hearing loss because she had worked many years in the New York school system, recommended that they go to Albert Einstein Medical Center in the Bronx. Bill and Jeanine arranged for a follow-up test a few weeks after Grace was born.

Grace failed her hearing test again. Jeanine realized she would need to educate herself about hearing loss and what Grace's options were. "It was absolutely devastating. You just can't - you can't believe it. You can't imagine your child missing all of that sound – missing everything. It is definitely extremely heartbreaking. And, it was definitely rough for those first few months coping with it and accepting it. And then you are hoping for a cure."

Jeanine did not want Grace missing out. When she thought of deaf people, all she was aware of was them talking with an odd voice and using sign language. Jeanine couldn't imagine that life for her child. "I'm an emotional person, so at times I was losing it. But, like I said we are action people. Eventually we plowed forward. There is nothing you can do but focus on, what can we do to help her?"

Bill, an engineer, went into problem solving mode, "I just remember a lot of tests. Within the first weeks the tests confirmed everything. You feel drained. Initially it's a shock. Then you move in to a stage almost like denial. Then it becomes, 'well okay if they are right, then boy what a disappointment.' After that you move on beyond the disappointment to accepting it for what it is. I'm a little different than most people. I realized we've got to put that all behind us, and keep moving forward. That's my analytical mindset. Give me a diagnosis. Tell me what it is and then let's figure out which way we're going. You realize there's really nothing that you can do to fix it. There's nothing that you can do to change it. So, if you can't fix it or repair it, what can you do? Then you start to think, what does the future hold? You have no idea at that point. It was scary to think about her life and how it will be. At the same time, it was hard to really think too far ahead."

Although Jeanine's reaction was more emotional than Bill's, they both focused on how they could take action to help Grace. "It was very difficult for Jeanine. It was extremely upsetting and emotional for both us," Bill said.

"Bill put up a strong front for me," Jeanine said, but there were sometimes when we would talk at nighttime, and I could tell he was upset, but trying not to show it and upset me. You want to protect each other. You know that the other person is upset, so you try to hold back your feelings a little bit because you know that it is going to make them more upset."

BABY STEPS

"At first, we didn't even know that there are different levels of deafness. We just knew the word 'deaf' - and someone that is deaf couldn't hear. We didn't know there were different levels - mild loss, moderate loss - or severe loss and profound loss. There is such a huge learning curve. There was so much going on those first few months."

After their initial hospital screening, many children with hearing loss fall through the cracks because their parents or doctor may not recognize the severity of the problem. They aren't diagnosed until a few years later when it becomes noticeable that they don't hear properly or have severe speech and language delays. Jeanine and Bill were not going to let that happen. Jeanine and Bill took a 21-day-old Grace for a follow-up test called Auditory Brainstem Response, which can be performed when the baby is resting or sleeping.

They followed up with visits to a genetic counselor, an ENT, and an audiologist to better diagnose the hearing loss. This was the first step towards early intervention services for Grace's hearing loss and language stimulation needs. It was overwhelming for Jeanine and Bill.

Jeanine realized they had to get past those feelings and focus on helping Grace. "We still had a long way to go on the learning curve for raising a child with a physical disability, but we were moving forward and we were determined Grace would have a wonderful life ahead of her. We have never considered Grace disabled."

When Grace was four months old, Jeanine and Bill took Grace to Montefiore Medical Center in the Bronx for further hearing evaluations as her family friend had suggested. Jeanine was born in the Bronx, so family and friends there pitched in to help.

"My parents and brothers lived in the Tristate area. They knew there wasn't anything they could do to change the situation, but they would watch Shain and Luke when we went to the doctors. I know everyone in both of our families felt better that they were helping in some way. I know they felt kind of helpless knowing that with Grace's hearing loss there really was no way to cure it."

The ENT checked for possible damage to Grace's middle ears and had an MRI done. The tests revealed that Grace did not have a conductive hearing loss, which in some cases can be corrected with surgery. Instead she had a "congenital bilateral moderately severe sensorineural hearing loss." This means she was born with an inner ear hearing loss in both ears. Unlike many conductive hearing loss cases, there is no "cure" for this type of hearing loss.

"Moderately severe" meant that Grace could hear sounds like a dog barking, piano playing, or a lawn mower nearby. But, when she heard those sounds it would be at the same level as a whisper. She couldn't hear people talking – and what little she did would be unintelligible.

That meant without proper amplification and intervention from hearing aids, Grace would find it extremely difficult to learn to speak or understand others speaking. Without hearing aids, she would miss what her teachers and fellow students were saying when she went to school.

Grace's ENT, Dr. Francis Deane, was in Jeanine and Bill's health insurance network, so his fees were fully covered. He was a wonderful, kind man who would quack and talk like Donald Duck for the kids. He was planning on retiring, so he referred them Dr. Simon Parisier, who was renowned for his work in pediatric hearing loss.

The Gleba family made another trip to New York City in August to see Dr. Parisier at Lenox Hill Hospital for a complete evaluation. Jeanine was grateful that Shain and Luke were on an adventure in Central Park with their grandfather and Uncle Doug while Grace was examined. The boys would have fun with the family while Jeanine and Bill could focus on Grace. "When you are faced with a challenge like this, you come to fully understand and appreciate the depth of support your family will provide, and all that they would do to help you. We continually received incredible unwavering help and support from both of our families no matter the distance on a map. We know how lucky we were that we had our family available to pitch in. At this point we were not ready to talk to the boys about Grace."

Dr. Parisier has been called a "Hearing Hero." He is considered a pioneer in the development of the cochlear implant. Cochlear implant surgery was relatively new in 1999, and not many children in the United States had it. Jeanine and Bill had heard it was a "miracle" for deaf children.

The entire family held out great hope that this doctor would be able to help Grace. Dr. Parisier again explained to Jeanine and Bill that Grace was not a candidate for a cochlear implant.

"We read about cochlear implants, and we were hopeful," Bill said. "They are surgically implanted electronic hearing devices. When we found Grace was not a candidate, it was discouraging."

The cochlear implant surgery destroys the cochlea, which is the sensory organ of hearing. So, any hearing Grace had would be lost. The surgery was best for children who had no hearing at all and who would not benefit from hearing aids.

Grace did not have a profound hearing loss – she had some hearing, which could be amplified with hearing aids. With hearing aids it would be possible for Grace to learn to hear and speak!

As a result, Dr. Parisier wrote a letter to Jeanine and Bill's insurance company. He explained that hearing aids were prescribed for Grace because they were <u>medically necessary</u> for Grace during the critical years of brain and language development. Jeanine and Bill were disappointed that there was no "miracle" for Grace, but optimistic that Grace would hear and thrive with hearing aids.

Before seeing Dr. Parisier, the Gleba's primary care physician had submitted a referral request for a non-participating provider, so they could see this renowned specialist. After a couple of weeks Jeanine received a denial to pay because Grace wasn't 18 months old, "the age for rehabilitation for a cochlear implant."

"Thank God we didn't wait till she was 18 months of age to see him and lose all those months of critical development - not to mention that she wasn't a candidate anyway for the implant given her type of hearing loss! When it came to children's hearing loss, our insurance company just didn't get it. Why wouldn't they want to help our child hear?"

SOUNDS EXPENSIVE

Jeanine and Bill had realized through their research and doctor visits that it was imperative for Grace to start getting sound to her brain. Jeanine had read on the New Jersey Division of Deaf and Hard of Hearing website that "every day lost is one more day of rehabilitation later." As hearing parents, Jeanine and Bill felt a great sense of urgency because they knew what she was missing in a hearing world.

Within days of seeing Dr. Parisier, they were back at the audiologist's office learning a new language with words and phrases like audiogram, tympanogram, decibels, ear molds, and gain from amplification.

"We also learned that unlike eyeglasses, which can restore sight to perfect 20/20 vision, hearing aids do not completely restore normal hearing," said Jeanine. "We were told that even with hearing aids Grace would still have a mild to moderate hearing loss. She would never be in the 'normal' range of hearing. This was a crushing blow and extremely disappointing news for both of us."

Jeanine had hoped with hearing aids Grace would hear like everyone else. "We sometimes forget what hearing must be like for her. It is hard work listening all day long, tuning in the important sounds and ignoring background noise. Sometimes she gets auditory fatigue. A person with hearing loss has to learn to filter out the noise and discriminate what is being said, so trying to communicate with others gets to be physically exhausting."

Expensive digital hearing aid technology was just breaking through at the time. Compared to analog hearing aids, digital hearing aids have less feedback and can filter background noise to achieve better sound quality.

Grace's audiologist recommended that Grace try the less expensive analog hearing aids for the first couple of months to see if she would even receive benefit from hearing aids. If that went well, she could get digital hearing aids.

Jeanine and Bill were shocked to see the sticker price of $700 each plus the cost of ongoing ear molds and batteries. The digital hearing aids would be $2,000 each. Jeanine thought, "Without the help of our health insurance, helping Grace would be a whole lot harder."

FIRST IMPRESSIONS

Grace's first visit to get impressions made for her hearing aids' ear molds was nerve wracking. The audiologist used an instrument to push a tiny piece of foam with a string attached into Grace's ear. The foam protected her ear as the audiologist used a syringe-like tool to squirt in a "Silly Putty" looking substance into her ear. Grace's head was not supposed to move as the substance hardened – a difficult task with this uncomfortable goop in her ears. After a few minutes, the impression was removed and used to make a custom mold for her behind-the-ear hearing aid.

For infants these molds need to be replaced every couple of months as they grow at a cost of about $150 per pair. Sometimes the molds didn't fit properly and the whole procedure had to be repeated. Without a proper fit, the hearing aids would feedback with a piercing, screeching, whistling sound.

On August 16, 1999, three-month-old Grace was fitted with her first pair of hearing aids. It was a day that will always be remembered in the Gleba household. The hearing aids looked so big on her tiny ears when Grace's audiologist, Giri, put them on her ears. Giri turned on the hearing aids as Jeanine was cradling Grace in her arms. With the push of a button, Grace heard her

Mom's voice saying, "Grace" – the very first word she ever heard. Grace started wailing - the unfamiliar sound scared her.

The tears fell from Jeanine's eyes. "I was momentarily even afraid to speak for fear it was hurting her. Giri immediately put her arm around me to comfort me and said, 'It's okay. Talk to her.' It was an incredible moment as I told my baby, 'Grace. It's okay. Mommy is here.' And, she could finally hear me."

In baby books there is always the major milestone "Baby's First Word." In Grace's baby book Jeanine and Bill added two new milestones "Baby's First Word **Heard**" and "First Hearing Aids."

"At first we were a little afraid the sound was hurting her because she was crying. We didn't know if it was too loud, or if it was hurting her. But the audiologist said that she was going to get used to it. Then I wanted her to hear everything for the first time, from music to voices – to everything. We had learned that the more a child hears people talk, the more she learns. So, we wanted her to hear everyone's voices especially Shain and Luke."

"That was so memorable and emotional because I had been trying not to keep dwelling on her not hearing every little sound. You could spiral into a depression that you would never get out of if you thought about it too much. I started remembering when I realized that while I was pregnant she couldn't hear me talking. And then I thought of her first three months at home not hearing us. When the hearing aids were turned on, the sound hit her, and then she started crying. That's when it really hit me hard that man this kid really couldn't hear. That's the whole denial part of it. You just can't imagine that your kid isn't really listening. Those first hearing aids were big, blocky and ugly. Even though they looked ridiculous, they were giving her sound. The hearing aids were like little miracles. And the realization came over me how these things might mean my child could hear and speak. It was the biggest moment ever. They turned those hearing aids on, and it was incredible," remembers Jeanine.

They left Giri's office after providing their primary doctor's prescription and paying for the hearing aids, which they planned to submit as a claim to their insurance company.

Jeanine would eventually visit the audiologist every three months until Grace turned six. After that, it was every six months for hearing tests and ear molds.

Every trip, Shain and Luke would accompany Grace and Jeanine on the two-hour round-trip drive and wait patiently in the waiting room. "In those early years there were many visits, and I was grateful Luke was with me because he would make funny faces at Grace in the hopes of stopping her tears as her ears were being poked and prodded because he could not bear to see her crying. There are moments that were heart-breaking to everyone - even her three-year-old big brother. I was blessed with very patient, well-behaved little troopers. Also, an occasional trip to Burger King or an ice cream treat afterwards never hurt."

"After each visit when we tested her hearing I prayed it stayed the same and did not get worse. Although we had been told her hearing would never become 'normal' or get better, deep down I desperately hoped it would. However, instead of a treat for me on the journey home I said a silent prayer of thanks that her hearing had not fluctuated and that she was listening great with the hearing aids. Unless of course we were stuck in bumper-to-bumper traffic on Interstate 80. I was still thrilled Grace was doing so well, but sitting there going five miles per hour I couldn't help damning everything to hell."

KNOWLEDGE IS POWER

Those first three months were non-stop, and one of the most stressful times of Jeanine's life. In addition to all the doctor visits, accepting their child had been born with a hearing loss, and selecting and fitting hearing aids, Jeanine and Bill had to make a very critical decision for Grace's future that would affect their family every day.

Like all parents who learn their child has a hearing loss, Jeanine and Bill had to choose a "philosophy" - what mode of communication did they want Grace to have? The choices were all new to them - cued speech, sign language, aural language, auditory-verbal and total communication. Once they made their choice, they also had to find a deaf program in New Jersey that offered it.

Inspired by Thomas Jefferson's words that "knowledge is power" quoted to her from a friend, Jeanine began her research. She read books, searched the Internet, and she and Bill visited all the deaf programs in New Jersey. They felt the more information they had, the more intelligent of a decision they could make. There were so many options it felt overwhelming.

"My mother's friend, Mary Finn, was a speech therapist, and she gave me so much information about language and hearing. She is the one who taught me that 'knowledge is power' from the get go. She told us before you make any choices about dealing with Grace's future, you must be informed."

"Most books that I read and the professionals we met with offered the same options. But, none ever made an actual recommendation except to say, 'It is a personal choice. We can't tell you what to do.' Deep down Bill and I knew we wanted her to speak like everyone around her but would she be able to? Eventually two people were brave enough to tell it like it is even though as we all know there are no guarantees of anything in life."

Grace's audiologist Giri told Jeanine and Bill, "Do not ever say Grace is deaf. She is not deaf. She is hearing impaired. And, she can learn to talk. Contact the Summit Speech School." She

was the first person to "tell like it is" to Bill and
Jeanine.

"HERE CHILDREN LEARN TO LISTEN AND SPEAK FOR THEMSELVES"

That same month Jeanine and Bill made appointments to visit several schools including the Summit Speech School in New Providence, New Jersey - an hour away from their home. They learned that at Summit infants receive Early Intervention services from a teacher of the deaf who comes to your home. Grace would not actually go to a school until she was preschool age.

The Summit Speech School follows the "auditory-oral philosophy." Its slogan is, "where children learn to listen and speak for themselves." Only 40 such schools are in the United States, so Jeanine felt fortunate the school was only an hour away. "By this point we had been agonizing over making the right decision. Although we knew nothing was set in stone and we could always change our minds, we still wanted it to be right from the get-go."

At the school Jeanine and Bill watched a short video on the "auditory-oral philosophy" and toured the facilities. Then they met with Claire Kantor, the Executive Director of the school. After talking to Claire, Jeanine knew Summit Speech School was the right choice for Grace. "Claire Kantor just exuded confidence and possessed a wealth of knowledge. She would later prove to us that she was tough as nails and the greatest advocate for children with hearing loss. She offered no sympathy for our pain and no cures, but she gave us exactly what we needed: hope and light at the end of the tunnel. Others might argue that for some it is false hope, but we knew Claire was not offering absolute guarantees."

Claire spoke frankly to Jeanine and Bill like Grace's audiologist Giri had, "Your daughter will talk. We live in a hearing world. Here she can learn to speak like her family and everyone else in the world."

"Claire could have been a great salesperson. We knew we weren't going to leave there until Claire convinced us Grace was going to go to that school. Claire gave you such confidence and hope that your child is going to be fine. Thinking that Grace would be able to listen and speak was incredible," said Jeanine.

Everything became crystal clear to Jeanine as she heard Claire's words. "Why was I torturing myself when I knew exactly what I wanted for my child...a voice of her own. Bill and I put our hopes and dreams for our baby girl and our faith in Claire and Summit Speech School. It was by far the best decision we ever made."

Bill agreed. "Over the first few months we listened to what the doctors and other professionals had to say, and through our research we had to quickly become experts without degrees ourselves so we could make decisions. The biggest decision was determining where she should go for help and what type of approach would be the most appropriate for her. We realized we had to trust our instincts. We had gone to other schools, and they were all great places. But, we felt best about Summit Speech School."

Claire made it clear that the auditory-oral approach, where Grace would learn to function in the hearing world, was their best option. "When we met with Summit's director Claire, she said 'if you put your daughter here, I guarantee you we will be able to make her speak and learn to hear as best she can.' Claire explained how important it is that a child's learning process starts very early. That is the time for her to learn how to listen and start taking advantage of whatever residual hearing she has left. Claire was adamant. We felt even if it didn't work out, then it didn't work out, but we had to try something. You can't predict the future."

Jeanine and Bill knew they were taking a risk – but they felt, what is life without taking risks? They knew there was a chance she might not benefit enough from hearing aids, which would make listening and learning to speak more difficult. They realized that sign language is the right choice for some children. Had Jeanine and Bill been Deaf and used sign language or if Grace had a hearing loss where hearing aids could not help, their decision may have been different.

Bill recalls, "Claire was tough, but Jeanine and I felt that she knew what she was talking about. Over time we got to know her. She was very strong willed. When she had told us Grace would learn how to talk, we had some trepidation. You wonder, how can that be? How do you know she will come here and learn to speak and hear? But, we realized we could either try it or resign ourselves to Grace having to sign. Signing is fine, but we felt if there was an alternative to explore, why not try it and see where it goes? If it works, well then, you have hit the jackpot."

Now Jeanine understood why so many people had told them that no one could make the decision for you and your child. "In the end it is an extremely personal choice, and you must do what is best for your child and your family. If you don't fully embrace the choice you made, you would be hard pressed to give it the one hundred percent commitment and dedication you need to see it through to fruition. I knew

Grace could learn to sign, but I didn't want her to use it as a crutch and for example, easily sign "water". I wanted her to tell me she wanted water. Our philosophy - or what quite frankly became our way of life - was that Grace would speak. And, we never looked back."

"It was tough to balance everything in our lives. We already had two children, and now we had new issues to face with Grace - as you would with any new child in the family," said Bill.

"We had to rely on the professionals, but I think faith played a part, too," he added. "Jeanine's faith helped her through it. She probably has a lot more faith maybe than I do. I tend to be more practical. We tried to make the best decisions we could. You hope you are making the right decision, and you pray that you are doing the right thing, doing the best thing, the correct thing."

By September 1999, Grace was fully aided with her hearing aids and enrolled in the Summit Speech School Early Intervention program. Grace's wonderful teacher of the deaf Nancy came to the Gleba home with her "bag of tricks" two hours a week every year until Grace turned three. Then Grace would enter Summit's preschool program.

"Grace's teacher Nancy did so much to help Grace and her support to me was invaluable," Jeanine said. "Since she was only with Grace two hours a week, and I was with Grace 24/7, she gave me the knowledge I needed to help Grace with identifying sounds, listening, and speaking."

"Nancy would come by each week," said Bill. "Jeanine was at home and I was working, so I couldn't be as involved as she was. I would try to come by as much as I could. Jeanine would help me learn how to help Grace. Nancy was really good. As soon as Grace got her hearing aids, Nancy started working with her. Seeing Grace's reactions is where we learned about how the brain clicks from the stimulation she was getting."

Grace was taught to learn through play activities. Grace and Jeanine spent many hours with Nancy playing anything from giving a doll a bath to baking muffins. All the while, modeling all of the language associated with it for Grace.

"I remember Grace having gigantic hearing aids on her head and all of the binders of information scattered in one of our rooms from all of her work," Luke said.

Bill and Jeanine had to learn to be teachers for Grace. It was hard to learn a new skill - to teach their child to hear. But they felt grateful they could take an active role in helping her – a big contrast to the helplessness they felt at first.

"It was a great feeling to know we could help Grace learn. It helped that I had a master's degree in elementary education. We always had a home environment where we stressed learning," Jeanine said.

"Jeanine and I learned that you had to face somebody with a hearing loss when you're speaking to them. Every child needs communication to learn, but children who are hearing impaired need more communication to overcome their hearing loss. They need to know more words and hear them more often," Bill said.

An activity as simple as a bath was filled with words for Grace to hear and learn - water, splash, soap, shampoo, dirty, clean, washcloth, towel, wet, dry, bathtub, faucet, hot, cold, all the body parts, rinse, and scrub. The Gleba's oldest child Shain was often in school when Nancy visited, but Luke was too young for school and often joined in the lessons. Together they created many "experience books" using photos showing Grace doing her play activities with the associated words.

"I remember Nancy testing Grace's hearing aids with the different vowel sounds oooo, aaahh, eeee like that," Luke said. "I remember my favorite thing that we used to play with Grace. Nancy had these plastic bears that looked like Gummy bears with cups. My mother told me they were called Counting Bears. We would sort them into the different colors. My mother ended up buying them to have in our house."

Bill remembers Shain pitching in, too, "Nancy helped the boys get involved. Shain was six so he was able to understand a little bit more, while Luke was only a couple years old and still learning himself. Shain would speak to her when he could and try to do the same things that he would see going on during the therapy session."

The family's "homework" also included playing music and encouraging Grace to listen. When she wasn't looking, Jeanine would stop the music, watch her reaction and ask her "Where did the music go?" Luke would play, too, and he would "freeze" when the music stopped.

In addition to Summit Speech School, Jeanine also enrolled in the John Tracy Clinic's correspondence course for parents of hearing-impaired children. Located in California, the John Tracy Clinic is an auditory oral school similar to Summit Speech School. The John Tracy Clinic provided additional activities for

Jeanine to do with Grace. Plus, the clinic provided personal correspondence and feedback after each lesson. It was another support vehicle for Jeanine where she could get advice at each stage of Grace's development. Jeanine also joined the Alexander Graham Bell Association for the Deaf and Hard of Hearing, which promotes the auditory oral philosophy.

The number one homework assignment for the Glebas was simply to talk more. "When you are a family of relatively quiet, shy people and not the most verbose this was quite a challenge," Jeanine said. "People who know Bill well know that he is man of a few words. I've always considered myself a wallflower in a room full of strangers. I am not the type of person who talks on the phone for a great length of time."

The Gleba family had to become aware of their environment and the sounds around them. Instead of setting the table for dinner in silence, Jeanine now had to describe verbally what she was doing as she did it. If the phone rang, instead of simply jumping up and running to answer it, she had to point out the sound, tell Grace what it was, and ask if she heard it. They also had to learn about managing background noise. They couldn't have the TV on when they talked to her. They all learned to concentrate on Grace when speaking with her.

"I had no room to complain as I'm sure it was nothing compared to hard work and frustration on Grace's part. Many times we would take for granted sounds in the background like the refrigerator's icemaker dropping ice. When she was young it would make her jump, but as she got older she would ask what it was."

The talking to help Grace learn applied to every aspect of daily life. It ensured that Grace would hear and learn the sounds around her and the language associated with it. At times Jeanine felt like a sports announcer on the radio, describing every detail of a baseball game for her listening audience.

It is overwhelming to think about every sound and every word, and at times it was exhausting to model language for Grace to learn. But, Jeanine had learned most language is acquired through incidental hearing – hearing the sounds of real life.

"Although it was intimidating to learn this, it ensured we talked more because we didn't want her to miss anything. We didn't talk in ridiculous amounts that it would seem unnatural. It eventually became a conscious act of speaking more or repeating or clarifying things that would otherwise seem obvious to a hearing person. Many nights I went to bed asking myself, 'Did I talk enough today?' But, we also eventually realized that while we needed to help Grace, she had to learn how to learn on her own."

By December 1999, Jeanine had written in her journal, "Without a doubt responding to my voice when I called her name. Made my day! Our whole family has seen a big difference in her. We are all able to carry on a conversation with her by going back and forth saying 'Aahh!'"

One of Jeanine's favorite entries read "I've even been in another room and have heard Shain initiating a conversation with her, which made me so happy because usually I have to prompt him. Now that he knows she'll respond he's noticing her more."

"I purchased a full-length mirror and did speech exercises on the floor in front of it with Grace," Jeanine said. "I would make simple sounds like ba-ba-or simply chat with her. If she tried to make sounds, I would imitate her. By nine months of age she was doing terrific and her language development was the same as a hearing nine-month-old. She was saying syllables like mama and dada. We were ecstatic! She would crack up with laughter whenever her brothers would make a funny sound or yell 'Boo!' She giggled so hard tears came to her eyes when her brothers did these sorts of silly things. It was great!"

"I wasn't expecting any immediate results with this whole talking thing. I knew from my education and my experience that children develop at different ages for all milestones," said Jeanine. For example, Shain started walking at 11 months, Luke at 14 months and Grace, the youngest, was 17 months! Same with talking - Shain spoke at 18 months and Luke 2 ½ years. The greatest irony of all, of my three children, Grace spoke first at age 13 months! Given the fact that both boys spoke later than 'normal,' had Grace not been diagnosed at birth I never would have suspected a hearing loss if she wasn't talking yet at those ages. I would have assumed she was a late bloomer like her brothers. So, it was a blessing that she was diagnosed at birth."

Furthermore, Jeanine describes, "From birds chirping and cats purring to music and words, we take no sound for granted. When we were eating Rice Crispies cereal Grace's eyes lit up as she exclaimed, 'I can hear it! It sounds like a fire.' And I replied, 'Yes, it does sound like the crackle of a fire!' Her ear was down so low her hair was practically in the milk while she listened. But by God she heard the infamous 'Snap! Crackle! Pop!' It was sheer joy to experience it with her. People take for granted so many things. While many people 'take time to smell the flowers,' we prefer to take time to hear the sounds around us."

Shain remembers, "It was weird at first. When she was a baby, I would say something, and she wouldn't hear it. I didn't really fully comprehend it. It wasn't that she wasn't trying to listen. She didn't have her hearing aids yet. Once she had them you would never know that she has a problem. To me she was just a normal person so I never really thought about it. You grow accustomed to it, and then you don't even notice it."

While Grace required extra attention, Jeanine and Bill always made an effort to make sure all the children got the attention they needed. "Over the years I have done my best to keep a sense of normalcy and sanity and above all ensure a sense of fairness. All three children receive the same respect, love and attention even though at times Grace required an extra helping of attention. I have never wanted her hearing loss to define who she is. She is a normal kid who happens to wear hearing aids like I happen to wear eyeglasses. I feel it is imperative that she knows exactly what is acceptable behavior and the consequences for poor behavior. The last thing we need is a spoiled brat and furthermore, how does this benefit her socially in her teen years with peers? Bottom line we are just as strict with her as her brothers."

Bill felt the same way, "Children need to know your expectations – what they can and cannot do. We decided Grace's hearing loss wasn't going to hold her back or be an excuse for bad behavior. As she got older, she had to learn how to tow the line like her brothers. We knew she would have some special issues. That's fine, but your behavior is expected to be the same as everybody else. That's the way the world is, and you've got to be responsible for yourself."

"Going through this in the early years made us much closer - not that we were not close to begin with, said Bill. " Like anything else in this world, you can take things for granted. When you go through something like this, you spend a lot more time together. You are making important decisions about your child's life and our life together, too, including our careers. We reached a point where we knew that Grace had what she needed, and she was like anybody else contributing to normal family life. You learn that there are more important things in life like time and health."

FALLING ON DEAF EARS

After Grace was born, Jeanine had taken a 12-month maternity leave offered by her employer. Fortunately, she was allowed to keep her insurance. But when Jeanine submitted a health claim for Grace's hearing aids, it was denied. Jeanine could not believe it.

How could something as critical as hearing aids not be covered by insurance? Her plan covered prosthetics, wheelchairs, and even cochlear implants. But it only covered hearing aids if the hearing loss was due to an illness or injury.

"How could they deny Grace or any child the ability to hear just because they were born with a hearing loss? What made one situation worthy of coverage and another not? A hearing loss is devastating whether it's because of an accident, injury - or you are born with it," Jeanine thought.

Jeanine tried calling her insurance company numerous times with no response. Finally, she wrote her company's benefit plan administrator. She even copied the company's CEO and President of Human Resources. After explaining Grace's type of hearing loss, she simply asked for help.

Jeanine wrote, "Shock, denial, and sadness are understatements. We are struggling to accept the news that we have a permanently handicapped child. We are trying to deal with all the emotions associated with this sad news. With all this stress, the last thing we need to deal with is a health insurance company lacking in compassion and providing totally inadequate benefits for this disability. Without hearing aids a child can't communicate her needs, thoughts, ideas, or dreams."

Hearing aids can cost $2,000 or more per ear. Plus, children require new ear molds that cost about $120 every three months. Jeanine wrote, "I am begging you to help me. I am sick of the phone calls, denials, frustrations, and feeling helpless. I strongly believe my daughter has the right to be treated fairly and to receive benefits."

Jeanine hoped that the CEO himself might write back and apologize. But, that didn't happen. Jeanine started what would become a great deal of research about hearing aids and insurance company coverage. Many companies considered hearing aids to be "cosmetic" like plastic surgery - not a medical necessity.

Although the company's CEO, HR head, and plan administrator did not respond, eventually Jeanine got a letter saying the Grievance Committee had reviewed and denied her request for coverage. However, Jeanine could appeal its decision by responding within 60 days.

She wrote them and said the policy was discriminatory because it covered some hearing aids but not all of them. An appeal hearing was scheduled for the following month. Jeanine started preparing her case.-She found an example of a family that had appealed to get coverage for their daughter who was born deaf, and they had won.

Jeanine walked into the appeal hearing with Grace and her husband Bill, confident she had the documentation to win their case. It was intimidating to walk into a room full of people - most of them doctors. The moderator was a Registered Nurse. To Jeanine's surprise all of them were employees of the insurance company, and not one worked for her employer.

Jeanine started by saying that since this was an employer self-funded plan, someone from the company should be there. When Jeanine inquired about the absence of representatives of her employer, she was told that it was the insurance company employees' job to administer the plan and handle appeals. So, Jeanine simply asked, "Why aren't hearing aids for Grace covered by her insurance?" Their insurance company representative's answer, "Because your employer chose not to."

Jeanine and Bill asked if they had to prove that the hearing aids were a medical necessity. Bill said, "Every single specialist, every single doctor, every single audiologist, and every single technician said without hearing aids Grace will not be able to hear."

One of the doctors answered, "No one here disputes that. It just isn't covered because your employer chooses not to cover it." Jeanine tried to explain about pending legislation, how other states mandated coverage, and quoted Alexander Graham Bell. It didn't change their answer.

This was one of the most frustrating days in Jeanine's life. Bill had lost that day's pay, and they had driven an hour each way. A complete waste of time.

But, it was also a day that changed Jeanine's life. Jeanine didn't know it then, but she would soon become a "mom on a mission."

"CAREFUL CONSIDERATION"

Jeanine was shocked to realize that the decision-maker was not her insurance company but her employer. The irony was her employer was a major communications company with roots reaching back to Alexander Graham Bell, an advocate for the deaf.

A few days later Jeanine received a letter that explained after "careful consideration" her appeal was denied. Jeanine wrote a letter to the editor of her company newsletter hoping every single employee would learn of her situation. They never printed the letter.

Soon afterwards, the district manager of the health plan administration department called Jeanine. The manager said they were going to review the plan and possibly "credit" Jeanine. When Jeanine asked the manager to clarify what she meant, she said it simply meant she would notify Jeanine personally.

Adding to Jeanine's angst, her employer ran an ad in the Summit Street School Spring benefit ad book. Summit Speech School was where Grace and other hearing-impaired children learned to "speak for themselves." Her employer supported deaf education but not the deaf children of its employees. That added to Jeanine's anger, and fueled her to take action.

"The whole situation with her employer was a mess," Bill said. "The way they looked at it was that it was just another person looking for a handout. One of the HR executives told Jeanine, 'I'll buy the hearing aids myself' – because they wanted to make this issue go away. But, obviously he was missing the point completely. Of course, we did not accept his offer."

"I was mad as hell, but Jeanine was beyond that. We knew with the attitude we were dealing with from her employer, they were not going to budge. We had to deal with a bureaucracy that wasn't going to change for anybody unless somebody in government told them that they had to. We began to realize that probably the only way the insurance coverage was going to change was by changing the law. We actually brought Grace in her infant carrier to one of the appeals. But, there was no budging on their part because they didn't want to set a precedent. After that, the push of 'there's got to be a way to make this happen' became paramount. And, we realized it certainly was not going to be easy."

Making a bad situation worse, Jeanine found out she was being downsized. She took a severance package and decided to focus her time on her kids, especially helping Grace. But she also thought to herself, "I'll be damned if I'm done dealing with my corporate injustice."

At this point Jeanine had no idea how to file a disability discrimination case. But, that did not stop her.

A CASE OF DISCRIMINATION

After exhausting all the options with her insurance company and her employer, Jeanine found out she could file a complaint with the Equal Employment Opportunity Commission (EEOC). Her employer received notice of the disability discrimination charge against them. After charges were filed, Jeanine had to go through telephone interviews with the New Jersey Area Director as well as follow-up calls with the investigator of her case. Jeanine's employer received notification in November that her charge warranted an investigation by the EEOC.

At this point it became a bigger issue for Jeanine than only denying Grace coverage for her hearing aids. Jeanine felt she could not let this discrimination continue any longer for any employee. She was determined to defend deaf children and their constitutional rights. This was a role she never expected, but she knew in her heart it was the right choice.

Jeanine had learned there was a bill in Congress to require hearing aid coverage for all federal employees. She hoped when this law passed it might set the stage for other employers to follow. She contacted *Parents* magazine. The editor Sally Lee was sympathetic but did not cover the story. Jeanine was disappointed, but encouraged that Sally Lee wrote her that "moms like you make a difference."

Jeanine also realized that if it was this difficult to get a sympathetic magazine to run a story it would be even more difficult to persuade legislators to pass a law. But, that did not stop her from trying.

After submitting her complaint in June, her employer received notice of the charge against them in November. They had 30 days to respond. They denied any discrimination and asked that the complaint be dismissed.

Jeanine was having doubts, but she held firmly to her belief that since the company provided hearing aids for some employees and their families, this was a case of discrimination.

In December Jeanine got the answer she felt she deserved. She was with her father when the letter from the EEOC arrived.

The EEOC wrote, "Based on this analysis, we have determined that the evidence obtained during the investigation establishes a violation of the statute."

Her hands were shaking and tears were streaming down her face. Her father asked, "What's wrong?" Jeanine could only say through her tears, "I was right."

Jeanine had believed deep down that this huge corporation was wrong. To have her belief validated was overwhelming. "Finally, score one for the good guys," Jeanine exclaimed.

SPEECH PROGRESSION

Grace's receptive vocabulary was growing in leaps and bounds. By eighteen months of age she fully understood the word "No" and would stop what she was doing. Like other children she would not always obey.

The family's "homework" for Grace was also getting more advanced. Since she understood the question "Where is?" Jeanine or Bill would ask her, "Where is Shain?" or "Where is Luke?" and point so she would learn their names.

Jeanine recalls, "A fond memory from that time was Shain watching television and Grace looking at a magazine while loudly talking gibberish. Shain was exasperated. He turned to me and said, 'I wish she would stop talking, so I can hear the TV!' He had no idea the impact of his simple exclamation, but it was music to my ears because she was being so vocal! It was so great that she was making so many sounds and baby talking. It was a truly wonderful complaint about a hearing-impaired baby!"

Grace had learned what to do with a phone. When she played with her toy phone, she would imitate the family by putting it up to her ear and say "I" for "Hi." These language nuances were always on Jeanine's mind. "It took many years of speech therapy for Grace to not have initial and final deletions of sounds like the 'd' sound in past tense words. But within two weeks Grace was saying 'Hi' clear as a bell - and turning into quite the social butterfly!"

Grace received another terrific progress report from Summit Speech School. She was really starting to understand more and more. One day she had been playing with a train. When Jeanine asked Grace for it, she crawled over to where it was, picked it up, and brought it to her Mom. Grace was hearing and responding! Jeanine said, "I was so proud and confident that she was really listening and paying attention. As a parent of two hearing children I had taken hearing and responding for granted, but for us her progress was huge! It was also interesting to witness her when she didn't like what a person was saying. She would scream until the person stopped talking - especially if we told her 'No' to something. Now as only a rebellious teen can do she just turns off her hearing aids when she doesn't want to listen to you lecture."

There were times when Jeanine wished she could do the same – just shut out the voices saying "no" that did not understand the importance of helping parents afford to enable their children to hear.

THE COMMISSION

The response from the EEOC Commission was a major step forward, or so it seemed. The letter said the commission would try to eliminate the alleged unlawful practices through a process of conciliation. If a settlement could not be reached, Jeanine would be advised of possible court enforcement alternatives.

In March 2001, Jeanine received another letter from the EEOC. She was shocked to read a "Notice of Conciliation Failure." Her ex-employer was playing hardball and now the case was going to the EEOC legal unit for possible litigation. To add to Jeanine and Bill's stress, the expenses for Grace's unreimbursed hearing aids and ear molds were adding up.

The letter also said that if the EEOC decided not to pursue a civil action, it would issue a "Notice of Right to Sue," so Jeanine would be able to take her employer to court herself.

"I don't know what type of resolution I was expecting, but I certainly didn't expect what was staring me in the face," Jeanine said. "I couldn't believe it. I was told the Notice of Right to Sue entitled me to sue them on my own behalf. That was a big 'if.' I had hoped it wouldn't come to that. In the meantime, I was stuck waiting again. At this rate I thought I would be old and gray by the time I got a resolution."

In May Jeanine heard from one of the EEOC's senior trial attorneys assigned to her case. The attorney said, "Are you ready to fight?" Jeanine answered without hesitation, "Yes. I want to fight. I've been fighting this for over a year. I'm in it for the long run."

After months of telephone calls with the EEOC, Jeanine was getting frustrated with all the red tape. In September the national EEOC headquarters decided not to litigate the case. The EEOC informed Jeanine that as a result of investigating her charge for singling out Grace's congenital hearing loss the EEOC found out the company was also in violation for singling out the employees who lost their hearing as a result of old age. They decided age discrimination would make a better case than children's congenital defects.

Jeanine was fuming. The EEOC attorneys would have never learned about the age issue if they had not investigated her complaint. Adding to her anger, the EEOC did not let Jeanine respond to what she considered to be an unjust decision.

Jeanine thought, "What good is a federal agency if it's afraid to take on the big guys and fight for the rights of disabled children?"

Equally infuriating, Jeanine had filed a complaint with New Jersey's Division on Civil Rights agency, which had a work sharing agreement with the EEOC. They told Jeanine that they would not pursue the case because of the EEOC decision.

Despite her frustration, Jeanine was more determined than before to see this through. In October 2001 she contacted the Americans with Disabilities Act (ADA) organization. They advised her to seek a congressional inquiry. She wrote New Jersey legislators Senator Robert Torricelli and Congresswoman Marge Roukema, "My daughter and I are entitled to protection under ADA, and I want justice to be served!"

Both legislators responded promptly and followed through with the EEOC. In November 2001, Jeanine received her last letter from the EEOC saying it would not litigate her case. It was almost exactly a year to the day from when the EEOC confirmed that Jeanine and Grace had been discriminated against.

Jeanine thought, "A whole year I waited! For what?" Now Jeanine was as angry with the EEOC as her ex-employer.

Jeanine had 90 days to file a lawsuit, or she would lose the right to sue. It was during the winter holidays, and she didn't even have an attorney. Adding to Jeanine's anger, the EEOC said they couldn't obtain a settlement, but they did not tell Jeanine what they asked for or what her employer offered. Under the Freedom of Information act, Jeanine obtained copies of her employer's letters in response to the EEOC.

In February 2001, the company wrote the EEOC that the exclusion was based on insurance industry standards. However, in light of the EEOC determination they were willing to propose an amendment to extend coverage for hearing aids. They wrote that they expected to amend the plan to provide hearing aid benefits to all participants regardless of the cause of the hearing loss, and they requested that the charge be dismissed.

Reading this Jeanine became even more angry and disappointed. Since the EEOC dropped the case, her employer did not have to comply. Because the EEOC had not made a formal case, Jeanine's employer was able to ignore its promise to extend coverage.

Motherhood spent managing a two-year-old, four-year-old and eight-year-old consumed Jeanine's time, and so she didn't dwell on the outcome of the EEOC case. She focused on Grace's progress as her language and vocabulary kept improving. Jeanine was thrilled when Grace sang "Happy Bopee" for her Mom's birthday. Grace now was calling Shain by name. Jeanine remembers his face lighting up upon hearing that for the first time.

Most people probably would've dropped the case at this point. But, Jeanine couldn't let them get away with discriminating and denying people - particularly her child - from listening and speaking.

Jeanine knew that large companies like her employer don't give in. They wait for people to give up, and they count on people quitting because it's not worth the hassle. Jeanine knew she had to take a stand. Instead of dwelling on it, she took action. She started looking for a lawyer.

NOT AS EASY AS SHE THOUGHT

Jeanine thought obtaining a lawyer who specialized in employment law or discrimination would be a "piece of cake." Senator Torricelli had written Jeanine that; "Many plaintiff-side employment lawyers would be willing to take the case on a contingency basis." She started by contacting the New Jersey Protection and Advocacy Group, who are New Jersey's "designated protection and advocacy system for individuals with disabilities." She also contacted the National Association of the Deaf Law Center.

After they learned that Jeanine no longer worked for her employer, they told her it would be difficult to challenge them in court.

"Apparently, because we went ahead and purchased Grace's hearing aids as an infant and since she was doing so well with her speech and language development we couldn't seek any further punitive damages," Jeanine said. "But had she not been aided and had developmental delays as a result, we could have sued. Where were the lawyers, advocates and public defenders like in the movies and on TV who did what they did not for money but to help the little guy and fix injustices?"

She even drove an hour to meet a lawyer who knew sign language and specialized in serving deaf clients. Again, she was told that since she was no longer employed, the attorney would not take the case. The attorney did tell her that if Jeanine wanted to hire the firm for $200 per hour, they would try to negotiate the matter without filing a lawsuit. Jeanine thought, "If I can't afford hearing aids, how can I afford that?"

Finally, an attorney that Bill knew agreed to take the case - despite the fact that it was a long shot and there was no big money to be gained.

Over the next year depositions were taken and the motions filed against her ex-employer and the health insurer for discrimination. By November 2002, Jeanine was able to settle out of court with all charges and claims of wrongdoing dismissed. This story does not include the financial details, or company and insurer's names due to this agreement.

This private battle lasted the first 3 1/2 years of Grace's life. Ironically, the amount of money Jeanine's ex-employer spent on legal fees would have paid for Grace's hearing aids for life.

"Most people would've stopped here after having the monetary victory (to cover the aids) they had sought. I realized this was a larger issue than just helping Grace. I knew that I didn't want other parents to go through what Bill and I had to experience. I never planned on being an advocate." But Jeanine would not stand by and watch other children not have the opportunity to listen and reach their potential because their parents could not afford hearing aids.

"This was a quantum leap for us," Bill said. "It became clear that to fight this meant making it a bigger issue than just our one family's circumstances. To do that, you're going to need help because to change a law, legislators have to hear from multiple people. They're going to have to hear from organizations, and they are going to have to first be educated. As we found out, opponents are going to fight it with their own lobbies. To succeed we had to get enough people to change their minds about what they were being told from the other side. We didn't view this as political. It was about doing the right thing for children and their families."

"People make the decisions that they need to make for their particular situation," Bill said. "Things in life aren't one size fits all. Other people in similar circumstances may have made different decisions for their family. We had built a network of people who approached having a hearing-impaired child the same way we did - including sending Grace to Summit Speech School or any other type of school that offered that type of communication. We were fortunate because we were able to spend whatever needed to be spent to get whatever needed to be done for

Grace. But, we knew other parents were not always in that position. When we found out about the lack of coverage, we thought, how can that be? How is it that a child that can't hear can't have at least some type of access? Why aren't hearing aids covered when something like eyeglasses are? Jeanine realized these other kids might not be able to get what they need to learn and grow the way Grace had. So, that's when it all started. It was really never just about Grace in particular because at the end of the day we were going to find a way to pay for what she needed– but we knew other families might not be able to afford to do the same.

Jeanine explained, "One of the strongest arguments for Grace's Law was the financial burden on families. Yes, we were determined to get whatever Grace needed, but that was not easy for us to do. We were fortunate that we could save the money to get Grace's hearing aids unlike some families who can't afford them at all. 'Save' is the operative word and to save was at the expense of something else. I wasn't working. We were a single income family for many years. We sent the kids to Catholic school, which was a choice we made for the benefit of all our children, but was also a big expense that added to the financial burden."

"Then and now we always put aside money in the bank for Grace's hearing aids and ear molds.

When she was a baby and my family found out they cost thousands of dollars throughout her life, they wanted to have a big fundraiser. We declined the offer because we felt someday we might really need a fundraiser for tremendous extraordinary medical expenses."

"It was and is a financial sacrifice for our entire family. We never took fancy vacations. We drove our cars till they had over 260,000 miles. The kids learned frugality and that in most cases if they wanted something it would only be bought if on sale. We have always had to be cautious with money."

"I have a quote on a tile that has been said repeatedly to the kids over the years 'Happiness is wanting what you have not having what you want.' Yes, we are comfortable and middle class but we also know how to make do without."

"The same can be true for many single income families, but with Grace's hearing aid technology needs it was even more so for us. Needless to say, these things are sacrifices that are worth its weight in gold. "

A LOBBYIST IS BORN

During Jeanine's original legal battle, she had learned that back in 1999 a bill for hearing aid insurance coverage had been introduced into the New Jersey legislature. The New Jersey bill, which became known as Hearing Aid Insurance Legislation or HAIL, had been languishing in the state capital since then.

"At this point in early 2001 I really had no idea how a bill actually became law. I didn't know yet that thousands of bills were introduced in each legislative session and that New Jersey's enactment rate was only 2.7%. In other words, for every 100 bills introduced less than three became a law. Once I found this out I decided I was not going to let this bill be one of the 97% that did not pass!" explained Jeanine.

Carol Granaldi of the Hearing Loss Association of New Jersey served as a mentor for Jeanine. Carol encouraged Jeanine to "pester" the committee chairmen trying to pass HAIL. After 14 emails, 14 letters, and 14 telephone messages, Jeanine did not get a single response. Two months later after the legislature's summer break, she received a letter from one of the Senators who wrote "I am the prime sponsor of this legislation; therefore, you can count on my support." Jeanine's interpretation? Don't bother me anymore about this legislation.

In the fall of 2001 after 9/11 everything seemed to stop. Everything seemed so trivial compared to the loss of life from this attack on the United States. It hit Jeanine especially hard because she lost her cousin who was not only a vice president of a company based at the World Trade Center but was also a new mom of an 18-month-old and a three-month-old. Jeanine wondered how she could go on after such tragedy. But she knew that she and everyone else had to regain a sense of normalcy - and for her that meant continuing with her battle.

ATTENTION MUST BE PAID

As Jeanine's advocacy for Hearing Aid Insurance Legislation or "HAIL" became known, she was asked to represent the New Jersey Alexander Graham Bell chapter at a national advocacy conference in October 2001. This was one of the first steps toward becoming a "real" grassroots lobbyist. So soon after 9/11 and the loss of her cousin, Jeanine's heart was really not in it anymore. But, she knew it was a tremendous opportunity to meet with other ordinary citizens like her who had been able to get hearing aid legislation passed in their states. Jeanine knew this was the motivation she needed to continue.

The consensus at the conference was that it was best to focus first on legislation for children. It was a smaller population than adults who lost their hearing due to aging. Plus, hearing is critical for language development in babies and toddlers. The final words in her training session were "go get 'em" - that was exactly what Jeanine decided to do.

"Jeanine was able to pull a lot of people together and get them on the same page," said Bill. "We spoke with Ben Dubin in Maryland, who was the president of the Alexander Graham Bell Association. He was very instrumental in getting laws passed in other states. After the conference, we had conversations with him about how he got it done. We would try to use it like a blueprint from another successful operation and try to fit it to ours. We felt if it can be done somewhere, then it can be done anywhere. Jeanine had to sift through a lot of information to figure out which was the best path to take and what's going to have the most success."

"Sometimes you negotiate to what you can get - to at least get a foothold. Then the next individual or the next group of people will fight for adult coverage. We wanted the legislation to be for everybody, not only kids, but we knew that that was never going to happen. By focusing on children, we got people's attention," Bill said.

In January 2002, Jeanine met with the New Jersey AG Bell Board of Directors. They were supportive but not prepared to launch a full-blown advocacy campaign. Jeanine realized she would need do it herself.

Jeanine had sent a flyer to all the parents at Summit Speech School seeking their support. Loredana, one of the mothers with a child at the school, had been a legislative assistant to a New Jersey state senator for the prior eight years. Working with someone with inside knowledge of government made Jeanine feel confident that the legislation would pass - and would pass soon.

Jeanine knew the power of the media. When she had been fighting her ex-employer, she got coverage on the local ABC News in January 2000. The TV news story not only covered Jeanine and Grace's situation, it is also touched upon the pending legislation. Although it did not change the company's stance, the media exposure helped Jeanine get supporters including a blogger known as the "Hackensack/Hong Kong Housewife with Balls."

Jeanine began her media campaign. She wrote a letter to the editor of her local newspaper. Her mentor Carol Granaldi wrote a letter to the editor published in the *Asbury Park Press*, one of the largest circulation newspapers in the state. Jeanine's brother Chris posted a link to the Hong Kong Housewife's story on the Yahoo Financial Message Board to help get the story out to Corporate America.

When Jeanine met with the AG Bell Board of Directors, a Board member told her that she had sought the support of the HAIL legislation with the New Jersey Speech Language Hearing Association (NJSHA), whose lobbyist said the bill had a zero percent chance of passing.

The NJSHA lobbyist felt they could not overcome the insurance lobby in Trenton. Jeanine realized a couple letters to the editor was not going to be enough. She was going to have to push the bill through herself.

FINDING A BALANCE

In the midst of all this political activity, Jeanine had to find a way to balance taking care of her three young children while taking on the task of pushing the bill through. In the spring of 2002 Grace turned three. Like most three-year-old girls she drove her brothers crazy. "Shain be quiet. Grace turn talking to Mommy!" The boys could not get a word in edgewise.

Shain yelled back, "Do you think you could leave Mom alone for one minute? You know can I talk for a change? Forget it." And, he stormed out of the room.

These sibling battles over her attention made Jeanine realize that when Grace walked into a room she was often unaware of other conversations that may have been taking place because she didn't hear them. She wasn't interrupting on purpose. Jeanine realized she had to work on Grace's social awareness skills.

"My brother Luke and I would joke around and call her Princess Grace," Shain said. "What amazed me when I got older is that my parents were able to give my brother and me equal attention. Any sporting event that we had, they tried to show up especially with Luke who played a lot of sports. Any time I did something like run for student council, you know my Mom was helping me. She was always able to juggle it pretty well. It's really an amazing feat because she was focusing all that time on Grace. But, at the same time with any effort she put into Grace's life she was also putting equal effort into my brother and me. Juggling all three of us was really impressive."

"We always had the same high expectations for all three children," said Jeanine. "We never said Grace couldn't do something because of her hearing loss. We feel Grace received minimal special treatment, but her brothers would definitely argue otherwise. Luke would call her 'your princess Grace.' Maybe if there were any special treatment, it could be a result of the birth order - her being the baby of the family. In recent years we told the boys to stop calling her 'Princess,' so wise guy that Luke is he would address her as 'Leia' as in Princess Leia from Star Wars. And, in recent years simply 'Kate,'- Prince William's wife."

SCHOOL DAYS

In January 2000 Grace had been fitted with the more expensive digital hearing aids. Jeanine and Bill wanted her to have the latest technology to improve her hearing, but this depleted the family's savings. They felt the cost was well worth it as Grace's progress continued, with her clearly turning upon hearing her name and turning towards sounds like the doorbell and telephone.

Grace was crawling around with a few thousand dollars on her ears. Hearing aids are not waterproof, and sometimes Grace would pull them out to teethe on them. Other times she would toss them out of her stroller. Fortunately, her brother Luke appointed himself as guardian of the hearing aids, so they were always found.

Turning three was an important milestone because Grace was no longer eligible for Early Intervention services at home. It was very difficult for Jeanine and Grace to say good-bye to her teacher Nancy, who had taught Grace those first few years.

"Nancy was a lifeline. We couldn't wait for her to come each week. I always wished it was more than two hours a week. We would watch how she modeled language with Grace whether she was playing in the sand or drawing a picture.

When Grace was three and started going to Summit Speech School, it was a tough transition. You had the same person in your home every week for three years. You have a rapport, and then all of a sudden for that to stop was a hard adjustment for Grace and me," said Jeanine.

It was a whole new ball game for the Glebas. Their home school district would now be responsible for providing Grace with the necessary services and funding to ensure she received an appropriate education. Jeanine and Bill were concerned because by law, school districts are only required to give an "appropriate" education not the best and not necessarily what a parent wants. Grace would go through an evaluation process, which included social, psychological, cognitive, and speech/language tests. Jeanine and Bill visited the preschool disabled room in their town where Grace would be the only hearing-impaired student.

After the evaluations were completed, Jeanine went alone to the eligibility meeting to determine if Grace would receive services. She thought surely Grace would be eligible for services. At first, Jeanine was proud to hear that Grace had done well on her evaluation – until it dawned on her this was the district's way of getting out of providing the services Grace needed. This included paying for her to attend the out-of-district Summit Speech School.

As Jeanine's hands were shaking she calmly said, "I think we need to end this meeting, and I need to come back with someone else." As soon as she got home she called the Summit Speech School's Executive Director Claire Kantor. "Claire was tough when it came to defending hearing impaired children's right to attend the school and learn how to function in the hearing world. She was a true barracuda – in the best sense of that word. Claire made it clear that Grace had been medically diagnosed with a hearing loss and had to be classified. She told them our school district could not provide what Grace needed. I didn't have to utter a word. It was all Claire. That September Grace started the five-day preschool program at Summit Speech School. I learned a valuable lesson: you always need someone else in your corner that knows their stuff and can put it into the proper words."

The next challenge was transporting Grace to school each day. Although the school district would provide transportation for Grace to preschool, Jeanine and Bill did not feel comfortable putting their three-year old on a bus each day at 7:30 am to drive 50 miles each way with a total stranger. That led Jeanine to drive Grace 100 miles round-trip to school five days a week for two years. Jeanine would wait at the school while Grace was in class.

"For Grace a typical day now began at 7:30 with breakfast and hearing aid check, so that by 7:50 we were in the van and drove over 75 minutes to school with the daily inevitable rush hour traffic. Many mornings she would fall back asleep in the car. When she arrived at school, she was greeted by an aide and walked to the classroom. There were eleven students in the class with four teacher aides and a teacher of the deaf."

The students' day began with a project or free play while each child's hearing aid or cochlear implant was checked for good working order. Grace was then hooked up to a personal FM system, which was a transmitter that picked up the sound from a microphone worn by the teacher. It enabled the teacher's voice to go directly into Grace's hearing aids.

Like most other preschools the children took part in calendar time, counting, colors, shapes, weekly show and tell, snack time, outdoor play, music, art projects, and an occasional field trip.

During a language lesson a teacher of the deaf would use an auditory verbal technique where she would cover her mouth, so that the children would only rely on listening auditorily and not lip-read. Three times a week Grace was also pulled out of class to attend individual speech therapy. Each month the teacher would send home what topics would be covered, the vocabulary words that the family should emphasize at home, along with suggested and fun language activities.

"I had many opportunities to watch the class from the observation room and each time I was struck that most of the children in her class were completely deaf. It was a miracle that they were able to speak, sing, dance and laugh like every other child! When I would pick her up at 11:30 and she would come running to me with arms wide open, big smile upon her face and yelling, 'Mommy!' I knew this was where she should be."

GRACE'S LAW BECOMES GRACE'S LAW

In June 2002, a new bill had been introduced in New Jersey that called for insurance companies to cover hearing aids for newborns through 18 years. In September, Jeanine and Grace went to Trenton in favor of the bill. A local newspaper covered the story and interviewed Jeanine. The headline was "Mother of deaf child battles for coverage." Like most bills, this one did not move forward.

In October Jeanine found out another bill was being considered. One morning as Jeanine dropped Grace off at Summit Speech School on a Friday, the school director Claire Kantor approached her and told her there was going to be a vote on a hearing aid bill that Monday. Jeanine said she could never get to Trenton and back to school in time to pick up Grace. Claire told her to take Grace and head to Trenton to testify on behalf of the new bill. Claire said, "You need to be there. Take Grace with you."

Jeanine was a nervous wreck all weekend. What was she going to say? Would she have the courage to speak in front of a group of legislators. So, Jeanine and Grace made their way to Trenton on Monday morning - an hour's drive from home.

When Jeanine and Grace got there, Jeanine realized there was no one there to testify in favor of the bill except them. But the opposition was definitely present - the small business industry lobbyist and insurance lobbyist were there to testify against it.

When the chairperson called Jeanine's name, she went up and sat Grace on her lap. Nervous, she struggled to even turn on the microphone.

"I had been nervous all weekend," Jeanine remembers. "I had no idea what to even say. In high school when I had to give an oral book report my legs would visibly shake, and I was notorious for using 'ums' and 'ahs.' I decided to write down what I would say, so I would not forget any of my key points by reading from my speech. Meanwhile I had read my written testimony over and over again. I spoke it clear as a bell within the confines of my mind and in the comfort of my home. I was fully prepared to testify. However, the longer I sat in that room it became increasingly difficult to have the courage to speak in front of the legislators. These were the most powerful people in the state, and everyone in the audience was flashing legislative badges, wearing suits, and conferring. It was extremely intimidating. Even the room itself reeked of power and wealth with its beautiful mahogany wood furniture, crown molding, and rich colors."

Jeanine started reading her statement "I know full well the financial burden placed on young families and deaf adults. It can cost $4,000 for two hearing aids every 3 to 5 years plus the expense for ear molds and batteries. Thanks to newborn hearing screening my daughter Grace was diagnosed at birth with a severe hearing loss in both ears. She received early intervention services up until the age of three."

But, as she was speaking Jeanine was hearing a voice in her head, "This is your child you are talking about. This is your little girl who can't hear. These people are denying your child the opportunity to hear and speak."

Jeanine lost it as the pure raw emotion and the pain of having a deaf child came back to her. She thought about her child and other children like her depending on these people. There she was groveling in the state capital for help for all of them. As tears streamed down her mother's face, Grace said in her ear, "It's okay, Mommy." And, that just made Jeanine even more emotional.

Somehow Jeanine stumbled through her testimony, and the two of them returned to their seats. A moment later Jeanine was shocked to hear the Chair of the Committee Assemblyman Neil Cohen say, "I propose that this bill now be called 'Grace's Law' for the little girl in the room who spoke in favor of the bill." Committee members cast their vote, and it passed unanimously with applause! Somehow Jeanine found the words to express her gratitude as she walked out of the room with everyone offering their congratulations.

Now "Grace's Law" had a name. That was only the first of many steps Jeanine would need to take to actually get it passed into legislation.

Grace was too young to quite understand what happened. But Jeanine was overcome with joy. She called Bill and her parents from the car. She thought to herself that if one person has conviction, that one person could make a difference.

Shain remembers, "One time Mom was in Trenton testifying. She was telling a story, and she got really emotional up on the stand. People in the audience really started to understand that this was not just someone trying to make some money. It was a real problem that needed to be addressed."

"I felt that finally some people 'got it.' All I ever wanted was for my child and others like her to have the same opportunity as children with hearing - to level the playing field," recalls Jeanine.

"As Grace got older, she would let us know when she needed a new battery for her hearing aids. When she would wake up in the morning, the first thing she would do is ask us to put the hearing aids in for her. That was proof to me of how much my little girl wanted to hear. Knowing that, I couldn't stand by and let someone deny any child an opportunity to hear," said Jeanine.

HAIL OR HIGH WATER

In January 2003, Jeanine learned that the bill was one of many bottled up by the major political parties. "I learned quickly that the party currently in power had a huge influence on which bills ultimately got posted for votes and passed."

She forged ahead and continued to send out her "action alerts" that she had started sending out on a regular basis to an ever-growing list of people. Jeanine also began a list of action items to help raise awareness about the legislation. In addition to creating events, developing a public service announcement for TV, and trying to develop a slogan, Jeanine thought a celebrity sponsor might help get the word out. "When it is all said and done this disability is invisible and still does not have the attention that other disabilities or illnesses have."

Although there was no response from the celebrities, Jeanine's friend Loredana used a media contact to get publicity for the cause.

A news correspondent for New Jersey's largest FM radio station interviewed Jeanine and Assemblyman Donald Tucker, one of the bill's primary sponsors. Soon afterwards several New Jersey newspapers covered the story. One story referred to Grace as "the three-year-old

Washington, New Jersey, girl who has inspired a movement in New Jersey to require health insurers and Medicare to cover the cost of hearing devices."

The publicity paid off. Jeanine heard from the office of the Chair of the Assembly Appropriations Committee that the bill was at the top of her "to do" list. But she also said the state had been overwhelmed by its fiscal crisis.

The Lehigh Valley Express Times awarded the state legislature a "Turkey Award" and urged lawmakers to place the legislation on the fast track to passage. The newspaper noted that while insurers will pay up to $60,000 to cover the cost of cochlear implants, it didn't make sense not to pay the $2,000-$5,000 for hearing aids needed by children like Grace and others.

The Star-Ledger, the state's largest newspaper, sent a photographer to Summit Speech School to take pictures of Grace and her classmates. The Star Ledger's article said, "Gleba's activism has placed her at the center of a growing controversy over whether the state should dictate what insurance companies cover."

As the word got out more supporters contacted Jeanine. Even then US Senator Jon Corzine contacted her and offered his support. Jeanine felt like she was on her way to making this happen.

In the meantime, behind closed doors Assemblyman Neil Cohen negotiated with other Assemblypersons and insurance representatives. Now Grace's Law would be for children 15 and younger with a $1,000 reimbursement limit every 24 months. Jeanine recalls, "It was decided that with those limits it had a greater likelihood to get enough votes to be passed into law. I was quickly learning how the wheels of government worked, and I was frustrated that the citizens whom the bill impacted really had no say in the matter. I believe elected officials have a civic obligation to represent the citizenry of their state and that they have a moral obligation to speak on behalf of those without a voice regardless of whether they can vote for you or not."

ROADBLOCK BLUES

That spring one of the greatest roadblocks to getting the legislation passed was being built in Trenton – the MHBAC. As a result of New Jersey passing numerous state health benefit mandates on insurance companies, the New Jersey Mandated Health Benefits Advisory Commission or "MHBAC" was established. It took a year for the commission to be established and another year before it issued its first mandate review. That meant any pending bill - including Grace's Law - was stalled. In June, towards the end of the legislative session, Grace's Law was not posted for a vote.

Jeanine realized she had to change her strategy. Phone calls and letters were not enough. She had to meet the legislators face-to-face in order to persuade them to support the bill.

Jeanine was nervous after she arranged a meeting with an aide of Assemblywoman Bonnie Watson-Coleman. Her friend Carol told her that it is important to work with the aides to get things done. The aide told Jeanine the Assemblywoman supported the bill. So Jeanine wondered, why not post it? Then the aide told her, there were 235 other bills waiting to be posted.

The aide suggested contacting all the Appropriation Committee members. That's all Jeanine needed to hear. That September Jeanine began driving Grace to Summit Speech School for her last year there. Each day Jeanine waited at school for 2 1/2 hours while Grace attended class. Jeanine was already a volunteer at the school and eventually became a parent representative on the Board of Trustees. She also founded the school's Parent-Teacher Association and was its first president. Even with all that, passing Grace's Law became her sole obsession. Nothing was going to stop her.

That fall Grace answered a casting call for Toys-R-Us and was selected for the Toys-R-Us "differently-abled" catalog. The company had reached out to schools with disabilities in search of models. At age three she thoroughly enjoyed going to wardrobe as well as having the make-up artist and hair stylist get her ready for the photo shoot. As they left the photo shoot, they were told there was no guarantee that the toy she modeled would even end up in the catalog.

With the October release of the Toys-R-Us "Differently-Abled" toy catalog, the family was delighted to find Grace on the back cover. Jeanine's brother Doug used the ad as a postcard for his father to send to Assembly members.

The postcard said, "The image on the front of this note is from the back page of the Toys-R-Us "Differently-Abled" catalog. The little girl in this picture is our granddaughter Grace Gleba. She is the namesake of bill A3387, 'Grace's Law,' Toys-R-Us, a private company whose primary function is profit, recognizes the importance of special needs children. Shouldn't the NJ State Assembly, whose primary function is to represent their constituents, recognize these needs as well?"

November 2003 was an election-year for Assemblypersons and Senators. As soon as the election was over, Jeanine checked her list of sponsors against the election results. More than half the districts in New Jersey supported the bill. "In this particular instance it was a good thing that we had 'career' legislators even though there is always talk in New Jersey that the only way to fix our state problems is to remove many of these lifers."

Jeanine hit another roadblock when she found out that the bill required a fiscal estimate, which took another year for the fiscal estimate to be published. The total cost per year for New Jersey was $390,000. These estimates show what the bill will cost the state. Since Grace's Law amendments now covered the State Health Benefits plan (active and retired employees) as well as NJ Family Care for those who are uninsured, there was a price tag to the state. The analyst who did the estimate told Jeanine it was a small cost compared to the $1 billion spent a year on benefits by the state.

In December another surprise greeted the family. "We were even more thrilled to open the Sunday paper to find the first Holiday Toys-R-Us Big Book and subsequent weekly sales flyers with Grace's picture advertising the Leap Pad toy! It was awesome to think of everyone we knew drinking their morning coffee, flipping through their Sunday paper and spotting Grace in such a big-name catalog or thinking of all the kids across the country dreaming of Christmas and flipping through the catalog circling what they want and writing their letters to Santa. It will always be such a special Christmas memory."

In January 2004, the bill was introduced again and assigned a new bill number. Adding to Jeanine's frustration, because of legislative rules the process had to be started again from the beginning, including getting a new fiscal estimate. That wasn't the only obstacle. The insurance industry was lobbying against hearing aid coverage. The governor was trying to balance the budget and ordered his staff not to post any bills that would cost the state money. Plus, the election brought in new legislators that had to be convinced.

"Every year that would pass my anger would boil even more that the insurance industry would expand their coverage on things like Viagra while they still considered these hearing devices a luxury item. My anger strengthened my determination and my resolve to see this through to the end."

A legislative aide told Jeanine, "Do not give up. Keep doing what you're doing." Jeanine did not need to be told. The frustration and setbacks just motivated her more.

Motivating Jeanine was not only her love for Grace and her outrage of this unfairness, but the support of her family. "Thankfully, I wasn't the only person getting aggravated. My brother Doug's emails to the Assembly were forever giving them an earful," Jeanine said. Doug wrote:

Subject: REVISITING: "He that hath ears to hear, let him hear" – Mark IV:9

My sister is Grace Gleba's mother, the namesake of bill A3387. You people need some prodding. As it stands, you don't respond to email or traditional mail. If justice is blind, then the NJ State Legislature is deaf, because you certainly aren't hearing our message. So much for my so-called representation in Trenton.

How is it that the US Congress and Senate can create a bill to ban spam in a few months, have the President sign it in mid-December and the law goes into effect on January 1st, while in 2 years you people can't even POST a simple bill to the full assembly??? You people are a joke. The founding fathers would be ashamed of you. I hope someday my niece becomes governor and signs a law that takes away pensions from lazy, retired legislators.

Tonight, when you are getting ready for bed and tucking your children in, tell them you love them. Then get on your knees and thank God they can hear you! Sleep tight, my shameful leaders, then post Bill A3387 tomorrow!!!

Sincerely, Doug Williamson

In February Doug shared one of many letters he wrote to legislators with the Star Ledger newspaper, explaining this legislation was falling through the bureaucratic cracks. Providing hearing aids to children should be a "no brainer."

"Where I stuck with the facts of hearing loss, the legislation specifics and my family's personal plight in my letters, Doug struck other nerves to get our message across and give them reason to pause," Jeanine said. "God bless him for the almost infinite number of letters he wrote year after year for unbeknownst to him his letters were my perpetual hope."

Shain, 10 at the time, also got in on the action and took matters into his own hands. In March he wrote Governor McGreevey a letter stating, *"I think that it is great that kids can make a difference in the government. I am in the 5th grade. I read in Time for Kids about the state fruit and that you signed the bill. My little sister Grace Gleba has some hearing loss and needs hearing aids. My mother has been trying to get a law/bill passed known as Grace's Law. It will make insurance companies pay for her hearing aids. Will you sign that bill? If blueberries are important than so is helping a child with a disability."*

Shortly thereafter the governor resigned from his office after declaring himself a "gay American" causing controversy by appointing his unqualified lover to a position with Homeland Security.

That September Grace had started mainstream kindergarten in a class with her hearing peers. While every parent experiences the apprehension of sending their child off on their first day of Kindergarten, for Jeanine and Bill it was even more poignant. Grace had to catch a bus at 6:55 filled with kids up to eighth grade, and she didn't get home until 3:30.

Jeanine knew it was a long school day for any five-year-old let alone a child experiencing auditory fatigue by the end of the day. "When Grace set-off on the bus to St. Mary's, she was not hearing like the rest of them. Would she even hear the announcement at the end of the day to get back on this very same bus? The questions and concerns were endless. However, there was a deep sense of accomplishment and bitter sweetness. We had worked long and hard these past five years so that she could be able to get on a bus and go to the same school with her brothers."

"We knew mainstreaming Grace would be a tough transition – for all of us," said Bill. "Of course, we were concerned how other kids would treat her. I am not aware of any instance where she had an issue with somebody giving her hard time about the hearing aids. I know some of the kids get frustrated when she asks them to repeat what they said. It is frustrating for her, too, since she does not want to miss what people are saying. I don't know that anybody has ever really teased her or made fun of her. As Claire Kantor told us, she has learned to advocate for herself. She has learned to assert herself and that you've got to speak up. Otherwise, you are not going to be heard."

"Occasionally people will crack jokes about my hearing aids or deafness. I know it's not meant to be mean or offensive," said Grace. "What they say really is funny, and so I laugh with them. No one has ever done or said anything to make fun of me. People have always been very accepting of my disability. Even though sometimes I'm in an awkward or difficult situation not being able to hear as well as others, most people have made me feel comfortable. I've been one of the lucky ones. I wish there weren't mean girls or cruel boys who get joy out of picking on others and hurting feelings."

"When it comes to Grace's education, Jeanine has been the driving force. It is phenomenal how much effort they have put into it together. But the reward has been that Grace can function at her highest level possible. It was important to us that she was mainstreamed at a school where she could learn to fit in any environment. Just like working to pass Grace's Law, it is a testament to both Jeanine's and Grace's perseverance and persistence," said Bill.

A VOICE OF MY OWN

During the process of giving her daughter Grace a voice Jeanine was getting a voice of her own.

In March 2004, Jeanine had been hitting the pavement and starting to meet legislators in their offices, particularly the bill's primary sponsors Senator Bucco and Assemblyman Cohen. With Jeanine's efforts as a grassroots lobbyist came recognition. She spoke at the New Jersey Self-help for Hard of Hearing People Association's leadership training seminar. In five years she had gone from knowing nothing about deafness to teaching what she called "Hearing Loss 101." "I believe in the expression, 'If you're not part of the solution, then you become part of the problem.' I wanted to be a part of the solution," said Jeanine.

Jeanine kept making phone calls and writing letters. In May she wrote her first article for the publication "Volta Voices," which is the monthly magazine for the national Alexander Graham Bell organization. The article was aptly named "You've Got to Fight."

Later that year Jeanine received an award from AG Bell for her grassroots effort to help children who needed hearing aids. The New Jersey Health Care Quality Institute published its "2004 Annual Health Sense List" of New Jersey's most influential players in the political healthcare arena." Jeanine was excited because there in 50th place was - "The Testifying Mom."

Jeanine kept pushing, and she came up with a new tactic to give Grace's Law attention. She started by contacting St. Mary's School where Grace attended, and she asked that students be encouraged to write their legislators. With Jeanine's urging other schools soon joined the letter writing campaign.

Soon afterwards in May the Assembly Appropriations Committee posted Grace's Law for a vote. Jeanine sent out an action alert to her supporters and headed to Trenton to testify. She thought it might be her lucky day because it was May 27, Grace's birthday.

After waiting an hour in the committee chamber Jeanine couldn't believe it when the committee said the bill was being held and would not be heard that day. She didn't know if she wanted to scream or cry in frustration. Bill had taken a day off from work, and it was a waste of time for everyone that joined them in Trenton. Jeanine had no idea why the bill was being held up.

"Sometimes we would have to drop everything to get to Trenton because somebody decided that today we are going to have this on the agenda. Then, at the last minute they decided to cancel it. Then they would say, 'we are going to put it back on the agenda for next week. So, thanks for coming down to see us. You certainly got to see democracy in action," Bill said sarcastically.

Three weeks later, after more legislative delays, she found out Grace's Law passed the Appropriations Committee and the full assembly. Jeanine didn't realize it at the time, but this was a huge victory for the bill to be posted in front of the House. As she listened to the House vote online, she sat there pumping her arm in the air with every "yes" vote as the bill passed 77-2.

Jeanine thought. "Maybe this is it." But, it wasn't to be quite yet. In December she met with Senator Vitale and his legislative aide. The Senator said he was focused on New Jersey Family Care, which was dependent on the family's income. Jeanine responded that hearing aid coverage should be standard for children no matter the family's income. Then to make matters worse, she was told the bill had to be referred to the New Jersey Mandated Health Benefits Advisory Commission (MHBAC) and reviewed. That wasn't all - now they had introduced legislation to revise the MHBAC review process soon after they enacted its formation.

When Jeanine heard this news, she was not only shivering from the December cold but from the frustration welling inside her. It was the end of 2004 and a dead-end to accomplish her goal.

It would have made her life easier to give up, but Jeanine just couldn't. As she became better known for her work, parents started contacting her prior to spending thousands of dollars buying hearing aids to see if the legislation had passed. Jeanine knew what a financial hardship the hearing aids were. It broke her heart to tell these parents the bill was stalled.

"The biggest thing was trying to get the word out from a grassroots effort. You've got to realize much of this all came out of a computer in a few people's homes," said Bill.

Knowing how much hearing aids had changed Grace's life, she encouraged these parents not to wait for the legislation. Jeanine could not take the chance of any child going without hearing aids in the hope of financial aid from a law that might never be enacted.

Jeanine was moved by the response from the parents who contacted her. Many of them were going through the initial emotional turmoil that Jeanine and Bill had faced when they first learned of Grace's hearing loss.

One mother wrote, "It's so comforting to know we are not alone. I don't know you, but I am honored to have heard from you. I admire your strength and determination. Keep it up, and we will continue to rise and stand beside you."

With that kind of support, Jeanine knew she couldn't give up until she prevailed.

THE LOST YEARS

Jeanine thought of 2005 and 2006 as "the lost years." The legislation was in limbo. All she could do was call, write, and try to raise awareness. After Governor Jim McGreevy resigned, former Senator Codey became acting governor. "I was forever trying to keep up with what was happening in Trenton, tracking legislation and to be knowledgeable on legislators' priorities. In my own way I was developing the skills of a political strategist and analyst." In the meantime, Jeanine kept contacting New Jersey newspapers, radio stations, TV stations and New York news stations to get the word out.

On the bright side, in 2005 Grace joined the town's Washington Borough Redskins Football cheerleading squad. Just like their determination to pass Grace's Law, mom and daughter worked hard to help Grace succeed. At each practice Jeanine would write out the words for the cheers and the cheer moves. Then after each practice they came home and practiced more until she nailed each cheer down to perfection. They were both determined that Grace would keep up with the other girls who could hear.

When she was older she tried out for a competition squad. When the coach called after her tryout, Grace raced to the phone. With a kitchen fan buzzing loudly in the background, Grace thought she didn't make it because all she could hear the coach say was, "You tried your best and you were great." Grace felt terrible – until Jeanine was able to reach the coach and found out Grace made the squad.

Jeanine felt bad for her but she realized, "The important thing is that these little annoying nuisances that come with the territory of being a person with a disability don't stop her from going after want she wants in life. There truly are no limits for her - only those she puts in her own mind."

"When I tried out for competition cheerleading, there was some music," Grace said. "So, I learned to dance perfectly fine. Then they are like okay there is this drum beat that you should hear, and that's when you know to start counting and doing your moves. I couldn't hear that drum beat no matter how high they put the music, so my coach was nice enough to count for me because I couldn't hear."

"When Grace was a newborn and diagnosed with the severe hearing loss many dreams for our child seemed to be slammed closed in our faces," Jeanine said. "Quite frankly at the time we couldn't even fathom her learning to speak let alone becoming a cheerleader for a football team!

Needless to say, words cannot express the immeasurable pride and joy we experienced watching and hearing her hard work pay-off as she cheered at the games with a smile from ear to ear and how she inspired us. Unbeknownst to her many times there was a tear in my eye."

"At the same time, even if she never cheered again, it was a defining moment for me. I realized that this child of ours is going to be okay...better than okay. Sure, we will always wish she didn't need hearing aids. She herself has expressed this. But what life doesn't have its many ups and downs? What normal hearing person doesn't experience being misunderstood or communication problems with others? We all know with great hard work the rewards are sweeter and with Grace they are even more so."

"Grace is more outgoing than I am," Shain said. "Her cheerleading gave her a great social life because she made lots of friends. People really liked her and wanted to hang out with her. You'd never know she had a hearing problem because she was living a normal life like other kids."

Over the years Grace has been selected as Captain, broken two arms and cheered for Varsity in high school. She also competed at the UCA National Cheerleading Competition at the ESPN Wide World Sports arena in Orlando,

Florida. In middle school Grace also ran for student council president. She didn't win, but she was on student council for three years. "When I have my hearing aids in nobody thinks about my hearing them," Grace said. "They talk to me like I am a normal person. But, sometimes I need to take them out because of sports or cheerleading like if I am doing a flip. Then, they'll be talking, and I'm like 'sorry can you say that again?' Because they are so used to talking normally, they'll talk loud at first. But, gradually they go back down to their normal voice. Then I have to say 'say that again.' It can be frustrating at times. It does bother me when people say 'forget it' or 'whatever.' When people do that when I ask to repeat something, it sometimes makes me upset. It's not hard to speak a little louder when you are with me. I try not to let it get to me. It's their loss if they don't want to share the information kind of thing."

"Once my friends had a sleep over, and I took out my hearing aids because we were all going to bed. Then everyone was talking, but I couldn't hear them. They were asking me, if I could hear them. And, I was like, 'yeah sure.' Then I gave up on hearing them, and I just went to bed."

"Sometimes in school or when I am out, I'll see girls walking by, and they are staring at me and my hearing aids. I'm like 'whatever,' and I keep walking. This is the way I was born. There is nothing I can do about it, so I just got used to it."

"Grace being deaf has always been just a part of my life," Luke said. "I am always fearful of someone making fun of Grace. I would be the first person to defend her and teach the other person a lesson either through words or even physical contact if I had to."

"We always said when Grace was little that she could be a little tough," said Jeanine. "But, we felt maybe she is going to need that someday when she gets to school and possibly faces kids making fun of her. So, did she become a little thicker skinned because of her hearing loss? She might have been that way without it. I don't know. If she does get upset about her hearing loss, we talk about it. Sometimes it's heartbreaking. I don't cry when we talk about it. I try to encourage her, and pray to God I say the right thing to her. I can honestly say in many aspects of her life, her hearing loss has not stopped her. I really try not to let things stop her."

While Grace was progressing so quickly, there were many days Jeanine doubted that the law would pass. She would wake up questioning her efforts - were they a waste of time? Many times she wanted to throw in the towel, but it reached a point where she simply couldn't quit. "What kind of example would I set for my three children if I quit?" She wanted them to see that you shouldn't quit something because things are difficult. "You must fight for what you believe is right."

Jeanine had purchased a book about an author named Sarah Hale who persuaded President Lincoln to make Thanksgiving a national holiday. Reading the book *Thank You, Sarah: The Woman Who Saved Thanksgiving* inspired Jeanine to move forward. "Little did I know how much this little children's book would inspire me in my quest for Grace's Law. The first time I read it aloud I could barely get through it I was so choked up. I even wrote in the front cover of the book to Grace: 'We can empathize with Sarah. If she can fight for Thanksgiving, you and I can fight for Grace's Law! I am thankful for you every day. Like Sarah you make the world a better place.' It took Sarah Hale 38 years, thousands of letters and articles and countless bottles of ink, but she did it! She never quit! What was her secret weapon? A pen! She wrote and wrote and wrote until she persuaded people to make the world a better place." I read that book to Grace even when it wasn't Thanksgiving to motivate us to keep plugging along."

Whether Jeanine was writing a letter to her insurance company or writing to a legislator about Grace's Law, it wasn't only about her daughter. She knew the current state of hearing coverage was wrong. For Jeanine it was about principle.

Bill remembers, "There were times where Jeanine was discouraged, and she said, 'Maybe this is better off in somebody else's hands to follow up and run with it.' So many times it would start up and then it would die down. It was frustrating because every two years when there was an election, the legislators might change. So, you have potentially different people with different political affiliations. Some got re-elected, some died, and some got into trouble."

"It was an uphill battle that she was fighting, but she really stuck to her guns. At times I think Jeanine felt like 'I've given this everything I can. I can't do anything more.' There were times when you feel like you can't keep doing the same thing year after year. Eventually they wear you down. It's attrition. She felt at times that if things didn't break she was close to calling it quits if she couldn't convince people to change their point of view and change in the law. Fortunately, people actually started listening."

"I remember the Thanksgiving book we always read about Sarah Hale writing all those letters to make it a holiday," said Luke. "She always reminded me of my Mom. My Mom taught us to never be content with average – just because most other states didn't have coverage didn't mean we shouldn't!"

In 2006 the legislative process began again. Grace's Law had been assigned a new bill number for what seemed like the umpteenth time. Now Jon Corzine had been elected governor. When he was a U.S. Senator, Corzine had expressed support for Grace's Law. That January Jeanine wrote her first letter to Corzine to get Grace's Law on his radar.

Fortunately, all the primary sponsors of Grace's Law had been reelected. The year started on a positive note. In March 2006, the Pension and Health Benefits Review Commission recommended enactment of the Senate version of Grace's Law since, "The bill provides needed hearing aids to schoolchildren, which in the long run will decrease health and societal costs associated with hearing impairment."

That month Jeanine again wrote to Senators Lance and Codey seeking their support. Senator Lance became a sponsor and Senator Codey wrote a personal note expressing his support.

Further helping the cause, the bill was spearheaded by Assemblyman Neil Cohen, who arranged for it to be sent to MHBAC for a study review, which cost $25,000. While the Assembly version of Grace's Law was being reviewed by the

MHBAC, the Senate version was sitting in the Senate Commerce Committee. Jeanine did some research and determined that the Chair of the Committee, Senator Gill, was actually the Senator for Grace's godfather, her brother Chris. Jeanine said, "We all know that a legislator's constituents have more pull than from someone in a different district. So, Chris jumped on the bandwagon and wrote a very persuasive and compelling letter to her requesting that Senator Gill post the bill in her committee. His description of me to the Senator put a smile on my face - 'My sister has a heart of gold and is a real-life super hero. She is one of the very special people in the world who never asks, but does and is a true, genuine, caring soul with tenacity of a pit bull to get good things done.' I never quite thought of myself as a pit bull, but I gladly took the compliment."

In May 2006, the MHBAC released its study. It didn't come to any conclusions. It did not make a recommendation on the passage of Grace's Law. It did not include any of the social and medical impact information required to pass a law. Jeanine immediately wrote to the Commission inquiring about this oversight. She did not get a response until January 2007.

Despite another delay there was one positive that came out of the study. It said based on its financial analysis that the impact on average health premiums for increased coverage for hearing aids would be less than .07% - about 20 cents per month. This confirmed what Jeanine knew all along. It would only cost pennies to provide this coverage for children who needed help with their hearing aids. "Finally, we had concrete evidence that this argument was based on inaccurate information. The mandates aren't increasing premiums as much as people are being led to believe. This had been increasingly used as a scare tactic by the business and insurance industries," said Jeanine.

The study was pivotal in getting the bill back on the legislative floor for a vote. In June Jeanine was back in the state capital testifying about Grace's Law to the Assembly. As a result, the law was passed on again to the Appropriations Committee.

MISS AMERICA

"Most years Grace and I would watch the Miss America pageant and write down our favorite contestants and winner choice," said Jeanine. "A few years before Grace was born, I remember when Shain was two years old we watched the pageant, cheered on the deaf Heather Whitestone, and cried genuine tears of joy when she won."

Years later Jeanine and Bill, who were always trying to stay current with regards to the latest goings-on in hearing loss, attended a conference in New York where the guest speaker was Heather Whitestone herself. "She was so gracious and possessed a rare endearing quality. Afterwards I was ecstatic to personally meet her and view her prized crown. Who would have thought because of having a child with a hearing loss I'd meet her in person years later?"

Heather signed one of her photos with "Follow your dreams," for Grace. Although over the years Jeanine had collected many autographs of celebrities, this was her most special and inspirational one.

"On a cold winter night in 2006 curled up in my bed under the warmth of our flannel blankets Grace and I watched the pageant. I told Grace all about Heather Whitestone. At the end of the show as we watched the new Miss America get crowned and wave, Grace who had since put on her own tiara, looked at me and said, 'I'm going to be her.' I told her go for it," said Jeanine.

POWER TO THE PEOPLE

Despite her progress Jeanine realized she still had to draw more attention to Grace's Law. She came up with the idea for an online petition to show New Jersey legislators that the bill was supported throughout New Jersey. Jeanine had learned that there were 720,000 deaf and hard of hearing people in New Jersey. She thought if she could get a few thousand signatures from her contacts in various deaf organizations and schools as well as reaching out to people who have hearing loss that it would help prove the worthiness of her cause.

In six months, she had over 1,700 signatures. She hoped for more, but it was a start.

Summer break came and Grace's Law was still stalled. Jeanine continued to reach out to members of the Senate Commerce Committee as well as the primary sponsors. A major turning point occurred in October when there was a surge in the number of petition signatures. Most of them said, "For Jake Whitenight." Jeanine didn't know who Jake was, but she wanted to get in touch with him to thank him. She tried Googling him but couldn't find anything.

A few days later the mystery was solved. Jeanine received an email from Jake's mother Lynn saying she was responsible for the latest surge in signatures. Jake was a two-month-old who like Grace was born with a hearing loss - as well as other health issues that would require numerous surgeries.

Lynn found out about Grace's Law and got Jeanine's contact information from Summit Speech School. Lynn wrote, "I'm very new to the cause, and I know you have been at it for a number of years. So, please tell me what is most effective, so I can apply myself forcefully in the right area. I've also sent a letter to every legislator in the state and to the governor. They will get a letter from me every day until I get a response from him or his office."

Lynn found out that not everything Jake needed to restore his hearing was covered by their insurance. She was as engaged and outraged as Jeanine had been. With Lynn's help Jeanine was able to spread the word even further.

Lynn had begun a fundraising campaign to help pay for Jake's surgeries. This included a flag football game in Manville, New Jersey. Lynn used the fundraiser to also raise awareness about Grace's Law. Eventually the petition reached almost 9,000 signatures.

In the meantime, Grace's love of American Girl dolls led her to an awareness campaign on her own. Grace had noticed that the doll's catalog included eyeglasses and wheelchairs but no hearing aids. Jeanine encouraged her to write the company and saw it as a teachable moment for Grace to advocate for herself.

Dear American Girl,

I love my American Girl doll! There's just one problem. She needs hearing aids like me. They are part of who I am and what makes me special. Just like some American girls wear eyeglasses to see many of us wear hearing aids to hear. Build-A-Bear makes hearing aids for the bears. Can you make hearing aids for my doll? I want other girls to see that it is ok to wear hearing aids because I am proud of who I am!"

That November she received a nice letter from customer service where they wrote "we are complimented by your confidence in us to create hearing aids for dolls"…and they realize "that girls want accessories and characters, to which they can relate and educate others as well"…"we sincerely appreciate requests such as yours as they help us to determine if we are meeting the needs of the girls we serve."

It didn't happen right away, but today the company offers hearing aids for the dolls. Advocacy and patience paid off.

SPEAKING OF EARS

Grace was 7 years old, and concerned with "important" besides the law – like getting her ears pierced. Like most young girls Grace could not wait to get her ears done. "I was concerned that she would draw even more attention to her ears and hearing aids with earrings," Jeanine said. "However, I'm no psychologist, but I thought if a girl who wore hearing aids wanted this fashion accessory, it was a positive sign that she was comfortable in her own skin regardless of her hearing loss! If she wasn't worried about it, then why should I?"

"I had special mother-daughter memories of getting my ears pierced, so I wanted it to be special for Grace and me. We used to read Judith Viorst's book 'Earrings' night after night. We went to a jewelry store where they pierced both her ears simultaneously. Grace, my mom, and I planned a 'Girls Day Out.' Grace asked repeatedly if it would hurt, and I was honest that it did pinch for a moment."

"When the jewelers pierced both ears, Grace jumped out of the seat with her baby blue eyes popping out her head from the pain! Then ever so slowly the tears started trickling down her rosy cheeks. Quite frankly she was in shock! She never dreamed the 'pinch' would hurt that much. Within 30 seconds my mother 'Nani' was crying with her! Fortunately, by the time Grace was slurping a milkshake in our local diner she was turning left and right admiring her new ears in the mirror wall."

However, despite daily care one of the earring posts became infected. Grace's skin grew back over the entire earring post, and it was very painful to remove. A few months later Grace tried again, but her ear became infected again. She was crushed.

"Much to my dismay months later she approached me again to get them pierced, and she even gave me her own money to pay for it! Unfortunately, her left ear would not accept an earring, but her right ear would. For years she only had one ear pierced, and she is never a day without earrings for fear that it will close up. All along I was worried that earrings would draw more attention to her ears and her hearing aids, but instead she got more comments from people informing her that she was missing or lost an earring because she only had one. Years later that other ear got pierced again, and she now has both ears pierced."

BACK TO THE GRIND

Jeanine needed to go back to work. She had been working as a substitute teacher since Grace entered school full time, but it simply wasn't enough money. Jeanine had read about the service called C-Print. As children with hearing loss get older they need help in the classroom. C-Print is a software program that enables children with hearing loss to have notes taken by an aide who accompanies them. After her training Jeanine started working with a student named Allie. They worked together for four years, helping to make Allie a success in school and creating a treasured lifelong friendship.

With Jeanine working full time, it became more difficult to devote her efforts to Grace's Law. If she had to go to Trenton, she would take a day without pay off from work. She would often take Grace from school so she could testify. While school was important, advocating for Grace's Law was too important a life lesson for her to miss.

Lynn had also told Jeanine she had gotten help from Paul Lavenhar, who volunteered at Summit Speech School doing public relations work. Lynn put Paul in touch with Jeanine.

The contact with Paul paid off. He advised Lynn and Jeanine about how to contact ABC and NBC news. Jeanine felt this was an added push to motivate the legislators.

As a result of these efforts ABC news reporter Nancy Cordes came to Jeanine's house to interview her family for a segment. This was not just a local story. The news producers realized that this was a story with national impact that should run nationwide. The ABC crew spent three hours at Jeanine's house for what ended up being a three-minute segment. The reporter interviewed Jeanine and her family, Lynn and her family, a representative from the New York League of Hard of Hearing, and the president of the National AG Bell Association K. Todd Houston.

On December 12, ABC "World News Tonight" with Charles Gibson aired a segment on Grace's Law. Jeanine hoped that this was going to change everything. Jeanine began to think that perhaps their effort would not only have an impact in New Jersey but possibly across the country.

Although the local ABC news channel had run a story about Jeanine's company not covering hearing aids when Grace was an infant, it was shocking to see the Grace's Law story on national TV. Jeanine's relatives from all over the country were able to watch it. But more importantly so were many people affected by the problem.

"When your family is getting publicity the way we did, I don't think you're ever really comfortable with it," Bill said. "We were fighting for a cause. We were seeking attention, but we had a goal and story to tell. As time went on, it became easier to do. We are not exactly folks that go out of our way looking for attention. We're pretty low-key, but we knew we had to get some momentum. Jeanine became more comfortable speaking with the media. I was not really included too much. We realized that the media wanted the focus of the story to be on Jeanine and Grace. That's what sold it to them – a determined mother making things happen for her child."

Jeanine started to get emails from people across the country. A grandmother from Colorado called to congratulate her on the story and offered her assistance. Jeanine was delighted that someone from outside New Jersey, who had experienced an insurance company denial of coverage for her grandson's wheelchair, was willing to help.

Jeanine was grateful that they didn't take a negative tone about the legislature. The story showed how important the legislation was. Soon after, Assemblyman Cohen called to say that he had seen the story. He was the only legislator to contact Jeanine after the airing of the show, and he promised to diligently work on getting the law passed.

ALL IN FAVOR SAY "AYE"

With one year left in the legislative session Jeanine and her supporters knew they had no time to waste. In January 2007, Lynn Whitenight came up with a new idea to publicize Grace's Law. She persuaded her local Town Council in Manville to pass a resolution supporting Grace's Law. She then sought to have the resolution passed in the other towns in the county. Jeanine followed up in her county, and it passed in her town Washington Borough and then Hackettstown and Oxford. Soon after her friend Carol got the resolution passed in Jackson Township. Within a year other mothers who supported Grace's law were able to get resolutions passed in Clifton and Washington Township. Jeanine wasn't sure how much impact resolutions would have on the legislators, but it was definitely raising awareness throughout the state.

As the Grace's Law momentum grew locally, Jeanine and Lynn continued to seek more TV coverage. In February Lynn wrote a letter to New York's News Channel 4, which resulted in a segment from reporter Michelle Melnick. The story included an interview with a spokesperson for America's Health Insurance Plans (AHIP). She said, "AHIP opposes the legislation and argues that mandating coverage of any benefit can backfire on the consumer. It is employers and consumers who pay the costs associated with added benefits."

Despite this opposition, the story was well received and continued to help make the case for Grace's Law. Soon after Arlene Romoff, the president of the New Jersey chapter of the Hearing Loss Association of America contacted Jeanine. She suggested that Jeanine contact the legislative sponsors directly and push for the bill to be posted for a vote. She also told Jeanine that she knew Assemblyman Cohen was devoted to children's causes and he was passionate about this issue. She said Cohen was Grace's Law's greatest advocate in Trenton. Jeanine felt lucky to have someone so dedicated to children supporting her so passionately.

"That spring we were like David and Goliath. The battle continued," said Jeanine. The bill was still not posted, so Jeanine's brother Doug sent messages to the governor and key legislators. Out of 20 legislators only Assemblywoman Marcia Karrow responded.

She wrote, "Although I sympathize and understand how much of a burden it is to purchase costly hearing aids, I have strong concerns about passing further health coverage mandates to the insurance industry since those costs will be passed along to employers and employees."

Jeanine realized she had to change tactics. To raise support about the issue, she needed to debunk the myth about the potential cost. That effort would start with a meeting she was able to arrange with Assemblywoman Karrow.

Jeanine was thrilled that the legislator was willing to have a one-on-one conversation with her. It was a chance to make a personal connection and "put a face" on Grace's Law. Jeanine talked to Paul who suggested trying to enlist the Assemblywoman as an ally instead of confronting her about her lack of support. He said Jeanine's underlying agenda should be to show the Assemblywoman how this could benefit her politically.

Nervous but excited, Jeanine and Grace met with the Assemblywoman and her assistant at a local diner. Over french fries and milkshakes Jeanine made her case.

Jeanine was impressed with how much homework the Assemblywoman did prior to their meeting. Jeanine gave her the fact sheet about the cost, a letter of support from Assemblyman Cohen, and details about the town resolutions.

After the meeting Jeanine took a picture of Grace and the Assemblywoman, which she sent to her. The Assemblywoman said she was one of the few politicians who would consider changing their minds about an issue. Jeanine asked her to be a sponsor of the bill, which would help make it more of a bipartisan effort, as there was only one Republican sponsor now. The Assemblywoman said she would guarantee at least an abstention, which is not voting either way. To Jeanine that was halfway to a yes vote. Encouraged by this response, Jeanine was motivated to keep pushing forward.

"I think very few people even understand let alone appreciate what it takes to pass a new law. I think people take for granted when a law has been passed. That may seem pretty easy. It's only easy if the people that are voting want it and work for it to happen," said Bill.

PATIENCE AND PERSEVERANCE

Jeanine was not the type of person who sought attention or accolades. But with her well-publicized effort to pass Grace's Law, they came anyway. As a result of her work, Jeanine became the first recipient of the Brian Shomo Parent Leadership Award, which acknowledges parents who excel in advocating for their children. Brian, who was deaf, had been the director of New Jersey's Division of Deaf and Hard of Hearing for many years. The award was created to honor his memory after he passed away in 2006.

In May, Bill, Jeanine, and the three kids attended the Family Learning Conference where Jeanine would receive her award. As Jeanine heard her introduction, she became emotional. "Not many parents are willing to step up to politicians and demand better opportunities for their children who have hearing loss. Such is the case with Mrs. Gleba. Hopefully once this law is passed, New Jersey can set an example for the rest of the country. While she may be an advocate and an expert, she is a parent first. It's important to demonstrate that parents can be both."

Jeanine's speech came from her heart. "For me it has always been the principle of the thing. It is the right thing to do for families who struggle financially and for people with this disability.

This was so evident to me after we were on *ABC World News Tonight*. A mother contacted me asking what she could do in her state because all four of her sons are hearing impaired. She had to choose which sons could have hearing aids because she could not afford to get them for all of her children. No parent should ever have to make that choice," she said.

"I think what our children accomplish each and every day is far more deserving of awards. Sure, I could easily have thrown in the towel and quit years ago, but what example is that teaching my children, particularly my daughter Grace? What comes so naturally to me just listening and talking is a constant effort for her. As a hearing parent I have no idea what it is like for her to wake up every day, put on her hearing aids, and live in a hearing world. Yet she never quits nor do I expect her to."

That November Assemblywoman Nellie Pou posted Grace's Law for a vote in the Appropriations Committee. Pou was chair of the Appropriations Committee, and Jeanine had contacted her many times via phone and letter to try to persuade her to post the bill for consideration. Jeanine was grateful her efforts had finally paid off. Getting through the Appropriations Committee was one of many steps required before the bill could become law. Before the vote, Assemblywoman Karrow greeted

Grace and Jeanine. Later that day Jeanine shared with her parents that Grace's Law passed out of the Appropriations Committee, and it was one step closer to becoming a reality. Jeanine was even more moved by the fact that Assemblywoman Karrow voted a resounding "yes." The Committee released the bill with a 10-1 vote and 1 abstention. That brought it one step closer to a final vote to make it the law.

Jeanine was grateful to Karrow. She was the lone Republican who went against the grain and did the right thing. "She didn't worry about the 'good old boys' in Trenton. This is the trait that common citizens want all politicians to possess when we select their name in the voting booth."

Her vote made Jeanine feel confident that they could finally make the law a reality. But could they do it in the last six weeks of the year before the legislative session ended? "I hoped we didn't start from scratch all over again in the next legislative session. I was beginning to feel like Bill Murray's character in "Groundhog Day" only I was actually aging and getting older."

"In my business life I have learned that the wheels of government turn slowly. Jeanine's experience certainly taught her that lesson, too," Bill said. "The biggest problem is you stop, start, stop, start. Trying to have a couple of hundred people to agree on something by a majority isn't easy."

Grace was now in third grade. One of her assignments was to write about her proudest moment. "I went to the State Capitol in Trenton, NJ to a 2:00 meeting to testify for a hearing aid bill. It didn't start until 2:30. A half hour, oh my gosh! We were so tired. At last the chairwoman came and then it started. I was extremely nervous when she said A289. It made me more nervous when we were first.

I told them that children need hearing aids. It is very important for kids, because they are my brothers and sisters. I want them to hear. We can make a difference in the world.

They all voted, but two of them said no. I was very disappointed. But at least everyone else voted yes and majority rules! I was very happy. My Assemblywoman told me she was proud of me and that I should be proud of myself. I am!"

BUILDING MOMENTUM

With limited time to move Grace's Law out of both Houses, Jeanine and her supporters again sought the power of the press to make their case. Jeanine's friend Carol Granaldi performed her own media blitz that resulted in editorials published in the Asbury Park Press, Trenton Times and the Division of Deaf and Hard of Hearing's Monthly Communicator. Carol told Jeanine, "I know this is a 'Hail Mary' but if we don't try – it's guaranteed that nothing will happen!"

Both Assemblymen Cohen and Roberts also issued press releases announcing Grace's Law had advanced and that Speaker Roberts would post it for an Assembly floor vote. Jeanine was relieved that Roberts was at last on board with her cause. Then another roadblock - the Pension Health and Benefits Commission voted "to not enact (Grace's Law) since it continues the unfavorable practice of mandating health benefits coverage."

Jeanine was not about to let this stop her. She wrote an Opinion Editorial for the Trenton Times entitled "Ring in the New Year." explaining that another legislation session was coming to an end and lawmakers were scrambling to push through their legislation along with the governor's priorities. Thousands of bills would need to be reintroduced in January 2008 and only a select few would actually become law.

"Grace's Law always remained a top priority in our household, and over the years she and I never missed a bill being heard for a vote and testifying. I would tell people that some people knit or collect stamps for a hobby. Getting this law passed was my pastime and hobby," said Jeanine.

Grace remembers, "I remember in third grade my mother started letting me choose to stay in school or go with her. I said, 'Heck no! I don't want to go to school. I'd rather go to Trenton and testify instead."

Unfortunately, because it did not pass before the end of the legislative term everything had to start over that January in the new legislative session. However, shortly after the New Year Senator Gill posted Grace's Law in the Commerce Committee - the first time the bill had ever been posted on the Senate side. Jeanine again rallied families and deaf adults to testify along with her, Grace and her son Luke at their side.

Jeanine had recently been in touch with hearing advocates in New Mexico who had successfully passed legislation similar to Grace's Law. They stressed to her that since New Jersey was in debt, it was important to justify the cost. When Jeanine testified, she emphasized that if insurance doesn't pay for children's hearing aids, taxpayers pay for the rehab costs for the rest of the child's educational career and later in life with the loss of productivity.

At the hearing Jeanine also said, "Since 1999 I have been lobbying for hearing aid insurance legislation. Since then ten other states have mandated coverage. Our goal is the adoption of a law that will alleviate the enormous financial burden on the families of children who are deaf or hard of hearing who are forced to endure inadequate insurance coverage for hearing aids. But more importantly, help give many children a voice of their own. Please hear us today."

Grace added, "Hello! My name is Grace Gleba. I am eight years old. I am in the third grade. I am here today to ask for your help in passing Grace's Law for New Jersey's deaf and hard of hearing kids...When I grow up I want to be a teacher. I will need to talk to students to teach them or if they ask me a question I could answer them. But only with my hearing aids on! We all have dreams for the future. Help make ours come true. Thank you for hearing me today."

Then Jeanine, her family, and friends held their breath waiting for the vote. The Republicans would not budge from their opposition stance.

As soon as Jeanine heard that first "no" vote, her heart sank. When it was Democrat Senator Lesniak's turn to vote, he addressed New Jersey State Senator Cardinale, who had issued the first no vote. "I agree with Senator Cardinale who believes that we need to set priorities. These children are my priority, and I think they should be our priorities. So, I vote yes!"

Finally, it was the Chair's vote and Democrat Senator Gill said, "Speaking about our children as offsets in a budget is difficult to take. We will continue the fight to garner the votes that are necessary because at the end of the day these children here are not offsets on some balance sheet on some political dispute, so I vote yes."

Jeanine, her family and friends were overjoyed when it passed in the committee. Senator Gill's words had inspired Jeanine and given her even more reason to persevere. Jeanine later learned that Senator Gill shared a law office with the bill's primary sponsor, Assemblyman Neil Cohen. So, she knew it was not a coincidence that the bill was finally posted in the Commerce Committee that she chaired. Assemblyman Cohen was a children's advocate who was in Grace's corner pushing to make her dream of making Grace's Law a reality.

In early February Jeanine received confirmation that Assemblyman Cohen would be posting

Grace's Law at the February Assembly Finance and Insurance Committee. It passed, and it moved onto the Budget and Appropriations Committees in each house. Again, Cohen was Grace's Law's "angel."

Jeanine kept pushing every button she could find to move the law forward. With Carol's help, she enlisted the help of the schools where some of her supporters' families attended. Students from all over the state wrote letters to Governor Corzine, the sponsors of the bill, and committee chairs urging them to pass Grace's Law.

"It was a combination of people - so many mothers, so many fathers and so many kids and then so many groups - that got the attention of the legislature," Bill said.

"I would keep Grace and Mom company going to Trenton, and I also testified," Luke said. "The more people we had the better. They would include me in the group pictures with all of the kids that would go to testify."

Jeanine also decided to follow the lead of the New Mexico parents who had hosted an Awareness Day to rally support. Jeanine turned to the bill's greatest supporter - Assemblyman Cohen – who readily agreed to attend and to have his name on the invitation.

Sadly, Claire Kantor died in 2003 at age 55 following a two-year battle with breast cancer. She had served as executive director of Summit Speech School for 21 years. Jeanine approached Summit Speech School's new Executive Director Dr. Pamela Paskowitz, who gave her blessing to use the school's facilities with an offer to help in any way possible. A press release about the event led to a front-page story in the local newspaper, "Family Urges Legislature to Give Each Child Chance to Hear."

Jeanine kept in close contact with Assemblyman Cohen about the game plan for passing Grace's Law. She wanted his advice from the perspective of a legislator. With Cohen's help, Jeanine had an additional ten co-sponsors – even more followed suit soon afterwards.

"We started getting a little more popular and a little bit more backing from the public," Bill said. "Folks were starting to call their legislators. We started getting word of mouth about our cause, or people would see something in the newspaper or on TV. People would get in touch with Jeanine and ask how they could help. Then the message started spreading out across the state. Over time more state assembly members and senators came onboard, and some became sponsors."

"As Jeanine got inquiries, they were able to slowly put each other in touch with even more supporters and the word was spread. It was a real grassroots effort. Their response helped us keep going because it confirmed, 'Hey we may actually have something of substance here.' We didn't want to let that go. Having that support encouraged us even more."

AN AFTERNOON OF HOPE AND INSPIRATION

When guests first walked into Summit Speech School for Awareness Day, Jeanine and her volunteers had set up display tables complete with balloons, flowers, and handouts. The school's young students who are deaf and hard of hearing led the Pledge of Allegiance.

Jeanine asked the audience to take particular note of these children with hearing loss letting their voices be heard. The children also helped present Certificates of Appreciation to the legislative sponsors of Grace's Law who attended the event. Assemblyman Cohen was the star of the day and pumped up the crowd to support Grace's Law. "One of my favorite memories is Assemblyman Cohen telling the legislators in the audience that he hopes to have this legislation signed before Grace goes to her high school prom! Since Grace was almost 9, I certainly hoped so."

A few weeks later in May, Jeanine's efforts paid off. Assemblywoman Pou posted Grace's Law for a vote in the Assembly Appropriations Committee. This was big news – Jeanine immediately sent out an Action Alert to recruit supporters to testify. Dr. Paskowitz sent Jeanine's Action Alert to all of the families from the school along with a personal note asking everyone for support. Jeanine's ally

Assemblyman Cohen personally called Dr. Paskowitz asking her to testify.

Supporters came from throughout New Jersey to testify – including mothers who drove for hours with their babies in their cars to speak their minds. The meeting room was standing room only.

Jeanine was the first person the Chairwoman asked to speak. Jeanine decided to change her strategy for her testimony. She felt like a general leading her troops to battle - fired up with her Grace's Law Army standing behind her. She physically felt the truth in the words, "We are stronger in numbers." With Luke and Grace by her side, she felt stronger and more determined than ever. Although Shain had to be in school and Bill at work, Jeanine knew they were right next to her in spirit.

"Madame Chair and esteemed legislators, thank you for posting bill A1571 and for the opportunity to speak in favor of this important piece of legislation, especially during Better Hearing and Speech Month.

I've stood before most of you a few times in the past. You've heard our story and why this legislation is needed, especially medically necessary for prelingually deaf children. Today I will be brief. I want to make one more point as we all get ready to celebrate over the holiday weekend and on Memorial Day honor and remember all those who fought and died to protect the rights and freedoms of American citizens.

The foundation of our government is built upon the words of the Declaration of Independence which states 'we hold these truths to be self-evident that all men are created equal, that they are endowed by their Creator with certain unalienable Rights, that among these are Life, Liberty, and the Pursuit of Happiness – that to secure these rights, Governments are instituted among men...'

We stand before you, our government, asking for your help to secure that every New Jersey child has equal access and equal opportunity: That they will not be deprived by exclusionary insurance policies the opportunity to alleviate their hearing loss. These kids have a Right to Freedom of Speech. Help them hear the sounds of Life and Pursue Happiness with this legislation. Thank you."

Grace was next in line to testify. Jeanine beamed with pride to hear her speak on behalf of all the children without a voice. Loud and clear as a bell Grace spoke the words, "Hi. My name is Grace Gleba. I am 8 years old. My future looks bright, but only if you help me and other NJ children who can't hear. I want them. I need them. I've got to have them. Hearing aids. Not in 2 years, 5 years or 10 years. I need them now. Every day for the rest of my life. To learn in school. To play with my friends. To be in the hearing world. Please pass A1571, this year 2008!" It was Grace's courage and confidence that inspired and encouraged the other children present to follow her lead and step up to the microphone after her and testify. Her story about dealing with hearing loss made it personal and real for the Assembly members.

Jeanine felt ecstatic when the bill passed and was headed to the full Assembly. With any luck it would be posted before the summer break.

When it was over, the personal stories of most of the families that testified were featured in their hometown newspapers. Each family became a local hero – and an advocate in the Grace's Law Army. Jeanine immediately put all of the press coverage on the website to continue to raise awareness.

ARMED AND DANGEROUS

In Jeanine's previous trips to Trenton to testify and watching the follow-up voting, it alarmed Jeanine that while a sign language interpreter or assistive listening devices were available upon request, Grace could not hear the legislators speak or vote.

Many times, they did not speak into the microphones, or they would look down. When it came to the end of a vote, Grace would look for the audience reaction – but she did not know if it passed or not. Jeanine added, "Grace would ask me "What did they say? What happened? Did they say yes?" This bothered me greatly. All this time she was missing the most important and best aspect of the whole proceeding. I only wish it had dawned on me sooner, but like most people who don't live with a hearing disability, I was oblivious."

For the June 9th Senate Budget and Appropriations vote, the "Grace's Law Army" was armed with individual signs on Popsicle sticks with "No" and "Yes" on either side. By this time, Grace was a nine-year old "veteran" speaker.

When Grace testified she said," "I have worn hearing aids since I was three months old. Without my hearing aids I can only hear very loud noises like a blow dryer or a vacuum cleaner. But with my hearing aids what a difference! I have learned to listen hard and can now speak in front of you. If I am close to sounds I can hear my cat meow, people laughing, my teacher in school, and my family and friends talking to me.

I have testified many times for Grace's Law, and I don't think the legislators know that when you vote on the bill, I can't hear you well because you are up there, and I am back here! My mother has always told me if we passed! So today I want to know right away, so please speak clearly into your microphone and look at us when you vote. If you want, you can hold up these signs for us to read, too. Hearing aids cost a lot of money. We need help to pay for them. Grace's Law is important to families and children who can't hear. Please vote yes today. Thank you for hearing me today!"

Grace proceeded to hand each legislator one of the handmade signs.

This committee meeting was one of the most meaningful and memorable to Jeanine. Committee member Senator Lance, who later became a New Jersey Congressman, spoke these words, which Jeanine framed for Grace, "Welcome, Grace. And I think it is very courageous of you to be here and that is true of the other young people that are with us. But considering the fact that this will be named after you for the rest of your life, you can be proud of what you personally have accomplished. There are very few people anywhere in America who have a law that is named after them. And here in New Jersey, Grace, the fact that this is sponsored by the Chair of the committee and co-sponsored by me as the ranking member on the other side of the aisle is an indication that you have brought the legislature together. I believe, Grace, that this will pass unanimously in both houses of the legislature, and Grace, next year we're going to put you in charge of the budget process!"

Moments later the senators voted and as each legislator spoke loud and clear into the microphone with a sign held high for all to see everyone's smiles grew wider - and Grace's eyes grew bigger as they learned it was a unanimous "yes" vote for bill S467 by all 13 Senators!

The shouts of joy and picture taking caused such a commotion that the meeting was paused momentarily, so that some of the legislators could join the family in the picture taking. They were getting closer to Grace's Law being passed.

As Jeanine drove home from Trenton this time it dawned on her that this could be it. The next step on the passage to law was a vote in front of the Houses. Jeanine knew she had to keep up the pressure to push Grace's Law to be passed.

With the coming summer break and both bills waiting for a vote in their respective Houses, Jeanine moved full speed ahead with plans to continue to raise awareness. Jeanine decided to form a team for the New Jersey Hearing Loss Association Walk4Hearing Walkathon in October to keep attention on the legislation.

CRASH AND BURN

Jeanine and her supporters were flying high with optimism. What could possibly go wrong? And in true Murphy's Law fashion not only did something go wrong - but it was a terrible wrong.

One hot late July Friday morning Jeanine got a phone call from her friend and Grace's Law photographer, Michael Kienzle, and without even saying hello he asked, "Did you read today's paper?" and when she replied "No", he said, "I think you better take a look at the front page of the Star-Ledger. It's not good."

Jeanine hung up the phone and went to read the news online that her "champion" and greatest supporter Assemblyman Cohen was being investigated for allegations of possession and distribution of child pornography using his legislative office computer. Jeanine was crushed.

According to the website NJ.com, on July, 2010, "A staffer in the Union Township office allegedly discovered a computer printout of a nude girl that was traced back to Assemblyman Cohen's computer. The two Democratic lawmakers who share the office with Cohen - Senator Raymond Lesniak and Assemblyman Joseph Cryan- then informed the Legislature's Office of Legislative

Services, which notified the Attorney General's Office.

"Both of us have known Neil Cohen for more than two decades," Lesniak and Cryan said. 'We know him as a compassionate, caring individual, but if the allegations prove true, clearly there was a side to him neither of us knew. We have been instructed to not make any further comments regarding this very serious matter. "

Jeanine could not believe it. With her mind reeling she was overcome by a whole host of emotions - shock, rage, disgust, betrayal, appalled, and finally sadness.

How could these allegations be true? What the hell had this man done? Breaking out in chills and shivering, all she could keep thinking of was the many children, most especially Grace, who had sat in Cohen's office, shook his hand, and had pictures taken with him two months earlier at the event at Summit Speech School.

It was mind-boggling that this was the same man who had been responsible for creating the law that provided a 24-hour hotline for members of the public to report computer crimes - including child pornography. Jeanine wondered, "What happened? What kind of monster was in our midst? What snaps inside of a person?"

Jeanine's phone was ringing off the hook for days and her email box was bombarded with messages from family members and all of the supporters of Grace's Law. People were sickened and repulsed.

Jeanine thought to herself, "We have a judicial system that is based on a man being innocent until proven guilty." She tried to hold onto her respect for Cohen and hoped that the accusations were false.

Despite her hopes, Cohen soon resigned from his Assembly position and sought psychiatric help. Formal charges were filed against him. In April 2010 he pleaded guilty to the charges.

"He not only betrayed any standard of decency, he betrayed the people of the State of New Jersey," Criminal Justice Director Stephen Taylor said after the court proceeding.

On November 5, 2010 NJ.com wrote, "Former Assemblyman Neil Cohen — pale, clinically depressed and barely speaking — was sentenced Thursday to five years in prison for viewing and printing photos of underage girls at his legislative office. Cohen, a Democrat who sponsored bills aimed at protecting children, pleaded guilty in April to a second-degree charge of child endangerment by distributing child pornography."

"What happened with Cohen was in some ways our worst moment. He had been fantastic. He probably had done more to help us pass Grace's Law than anyone else. It was shocking and disheartening. When we found that he got himself in trouble - that he actually did that – your first thought was, 'It just isn't the guy that we are dealing with.' But, unfortunately that's how it went. We realized we would have to start over again and find somebody else," Bill said.

For the rest of that summer Jeanine worried what this would mean for Grace's Law. Which legislator would take over the reins? Even more importantly, would the legislators still want to be even associated with this bill? Surely, they couldn't back away and turn on these kids now? She was beside herself. Was this how it was all going to end - with the bills just coming to a screeching halt and crashing and burning?

"Fortunately, after the incident with Cohen, there were finally so many people on the band wagon that couldn't understand how something like this could not be covered, that we had the momentum to keep going forward," Bill said. "Jeanine and Grace had gotten so many folks who wanted to be involved in the legislation that there was a strong enough coalition to pass it. The legislation focused on children, something that everybody could live with politically and from a budget standpoint."

Ultimately, Assemblyman Herb Conaway stood by Jeanine and Grace, and he came to their rescue. In the end Jeanine decided to do nothing differently. Assemblyman Cohen's actions did not take away from the importance and necessity of this legislation. So she proceeded with her course of action as if nothing happened – and she continued to gear up for the Walkathon.

Senator Buono reached out to Senator Codey in September specifically requesting that Grace's Law S467 be posted at the October 23rd voting session. Jeanine sent out an Action Alert with explicit requests to her "Army" to write to the Speaker of the House and Senate President. She stressed to everyone not to even mention Assemblyman Cohen. She told them to focus on the positive progress the bill had made that year.

The Walk4Hearing organizers were able to get the New Jersey Senate and the General Assembly to issue a "Joint Resolution for Walk4Hearing" to support the event. Although the sponsoring organization and Jeanine invited the legislators to join the walk, none did.

On a brisk fall morning on October 18th the supporters converged at the beautiful Mercer County Park now covered in colorful fall foliage to walk the 5K. Surrounded by her brothers and their families, Jeanine's heart swelled with pride.

Many of the families who helped to get this legislation passed, including the D'Alessio family who are still friends today, were in attendance. They were a sea of blue walking in waves with over 75 walkers - the largest team in the country that year - from babies to grandparents all blazing the trail for Grace's Law.

"I remember the Walk4Hearing and all of us walking together in our shirts and getting my face painted. Because of all the times my Mom and I spent together testifying, driving to Trenton and legislators' offices, and the Walk4Hearing, we became closer experiencing all these things together. I knew how much my Mom cared about me," said Grace.

**"Pint-sized 'Mr. Smith' Takes on Trenton'" –
Express Times headline 12/23/08**

A few days before Thanksgiving Jeanine received the New Jersey legislative bill subscription notification that Grace's Law was going to be posted in the Senate House. Jeanine was over the moon with elation! All was not lost!

Senator Lance arranged for Jeanine and her family to be on the floor for the vote. Unfortunately, with work commitments Bill could not join the family, but Jeanine pulled Shain, Luke, and Grace out of school to go to Trenton.

Jeanine had thought it was intimidating to be at a committee meeting with about eight Senators. This was a room full of 40 Senators! Jeanine was conflicted. She was happy that the vote was finally taking place, but also resentful that her hard work of so many years was in the hands of a select few.

She was quickly shaken out of her private thoughts and caught off guard when Senator Lance introduced Grace to the floor. He invited her over to his desk to give her the privilege of pushing his "yes" button. The Senators that were sitting behind were also very gracious to give Luke and Shain the same privilege.

"I still remember going for the big Senate vote, and we got to go on the floor and Senator Whelan let me push his yes button," Luke said.

Up on the wall was a big board similar to a scoreboard with the name of every senator. As each senator casts a vote the board lights up next to their name with either the no, yes, or abstain light. Jeanine was thrilled as every single "yes" lit up! It passed unanimously! Grace's Law was one step closer and one more final vote away from finally becoming a reality.

She couldn't believe it! Every single Democrat and Republican voted yes – followed by thunderous applause. Jeanine swelled with emotion as she thought of Grace hearing the applause with help from her hearing aids.

Jeanine couldn't drive home fast enough to send out a notice to everyone on her contact list, sharing the news and thanking everyone for his or her support.

A couple of weeks later Assemblywoman Karrow's office contacted Jeanine to let her know the Assembly bill was on the list for the next voting session. Better still she wrote that she would be honored if Grace would join her on the floor during the vote and "push" her button "Yes" in favor of Grace's Law.

Jeanine's family including her brothers and father were in the gallery for the final vote to make Grace's Law a reality. Jeanine said, "This time even Bill got to experience it first-hand. After watching our government in action in November and the subsequent excitement, I invited my family to join us up in the gallery to watch the vote and both my brothers and father were able to make it, too."

"The Assembly Chambers is as impressive as the Senate Chambers with its stained-glass lunettes and an enormous skylight that helps to light the bright and spacious hall. The tour description points out the gold leafing that decorates ornamental plaster work. A brightly painted wooden statue depicting the great seal of the State of New Jersey stands atop a high arch over the Assembly Speaker's dais and desk. We learned as we were being escorted to our seats by an aide some of the not-so-well-known details in the Assembly Chambers such as the carpet includes images weaved ever so subtly throughout all of it of some of our state symbols: the Purple Violet, the Eastern Goldfinch, the Red Oak Tree and Honeybee."

"We had to wait through numerous resolutions and proclamations before they even started voting on bills. Our immediate family was able to sit on the floor, but from my seat I had the perfect vantage point for seeing my extended family up in the gallery. My father would look down at me and after a most dramatic yawn and a roll of his eyes he would give me a wink or a thumbs up. My ever-impatient brother Chris was drumming away on the banister or furiously texting on his cell phone. Doug was calmly sitting tall giving me his confident reassuring grin that all was alright with the world."

On that Monday, December 15th – victory! The Assembly gave final approval to Grace's Law - with an overwhelming majority vote of 72 yes votes along with 1 abstention and 3 no votes. Next stop the Governor's desk and hopefully within the next 45 days it would be law once and for all!

"I knew we came full circle after 9 years when in the car ride home Grace said to us 'Do you know what I am going to miss most? Half days from school and being able to speak here.' "

"I shared the link for the proceedings online with our family members across the country. I knew it was big when my brother Chris started forwarding the link and subsequent newspaper articles to people saying 'Big sis...kickin' ass and taking no prisoners.'

Then he seriously wrote, "I am so proud. I really am...the fact I can let people know my sister with a 'never say die attitude' had a law passed and made a real difference in life. It's really humbling to know what you've done over the past many years. You have come so far to potentially make a significant impact on people's lives for generations to come when this law finally gets passed. It is awe-inspiring. Bravo!"

"That's when it finally hit me that this wasn't just helping today's children, but even generations to come. It was very humbling," said Jeanine.

The next few weeks were a whirlwind with all of the holiday festivities and subsequent press interviews for Grace's Law. Again New Jersey's largest daily newspaper, The Star-Ledger, wanted to run a feature story on it, and they even sent a photographer to take pictures of Grace at her dance class.

"We were all part of it, but removed from it at the same time because it was really my Mom's struggle with her pushing to pass the law," remembers Shain. "When it finally happened, we were all ecstatic. For her to have this victory after nine years - we were all just kind of in shock. After years of things getting done at such a slow pace and then for it to finally happen- it was amazing."

When Jeanine opened the paper on December 23 and read The Express Times editorial, it reminded her of the famous story "Yes, Virginia there is a Santa Claus." The headline read, "Pint-sized 'Mr. Smith Takes on Trenton"

The editorial said, *"For a little girl, she sure can make a lot of noise. Thank goodness for little girls with strong voices and the power to persuade grown men and women to do the right thing. Thank goodness for 9-year-old Grace Gleba. Born with congenital hearing loss, she became a vocal advocate for child-friendly hearing-aid insurance legislation in her home state of New Jersey when she was old enough to join her mother, Jeanine, on the stump.*

Jeanine Gleba has been lobbying lawmakers in Trenton for years after discovering that most insurance companies do not cover – not even partially – the cost of hearing aids for young children. Along the way she ran into quite a few brick walls. But she refused to give up, fighting not just for her own daughter – who was fitted for her first hearing aid at 3 months old after her family managed to scrape together the money – but for every hearing-impaired child in the Garden State. Last week persistence paid off for this Washington mother and daughter....

She's a real-life "Mr. Smith" in a pint-sized package. And while she didn't take on Washington, D.C., she took on Trenton – and won....so thanks to a spunky little girl and her mother from Warren County, hearing-impaired children across the state have a much greater chance of getting the equipment they need." How Jeanine's heart swelled with pride!

"Going through what we did with Grace's Law opened up a whole other avenue of life," said Bill. "Our circumstances with Grace led us to the situation that otherwise would not have happened. We learned a lot, and met a lot of people dedicated to that whole realm of bringing deaf and hard of hearing children into the hearing world. You can't even begin to appreciate it unless you've seen them in action."

He added, "Over time Jeanine became much more confident, much more an advocate, and much more educated about how to manage what she was doing. I think it changed all of us. We soon realized we couldn't think about this in terms of months. We had to think about it in terms of years. When I think about the change in Jeanine, it-wasn't something that you could see month to month. It was year to year. In a way I think we became much more cynical about a lot of things. But, you also learn what's important in life and what isn't important."

For Christmas Jeanine's son Luke gave her a beautiful painted tile inscribed, "She believed she could, so she did." His note said, "You have done a great job on Grace's Law that is why I got you this. I knew you believed in yourself to get to this point in Grace's Law. You have gotten to a spot with a bill that most people can't do in a lifetime. You rock! Love, Luke"

Shain saw how this experience changed his Mom. "This experience made Mom see the faults in the system - the faults in our government and how significant things needed to be changed. The experience with insurance companies really opened her eyes and my eyes, too. I think that it changed her because now she's an advocate for it, and she is really pushing to make sure that people will have this coverage. Now she's involved in local politics - and all politics starts at the local level. I think that's kind of given her a new outlook on life."

Jeanine thought to herself, "This was the greatest lesson I hoped my children learned - and learn it they did - quitters never prosper. At the end of the day there is much to be said for dedication and persistence."

"I am proud of my Mom a lot," Luke said. "I'm proud of my sister and everybody who lives with a disability. God makes each of us unique and we should try to make all of our imperfections blessings not curses. My mom is a workhorse. I wouldn't expect anything less. I learned the power of perseverance, willpower and most importantly the strength of a pen. All we needed after it passed the legislature was one signature on a piece of paper to make it a law."

A BELATED CHRISTMAS PRESENT

High on Christmas cookies and candy canes on December 26th, Jeanine and her family drove to Florida for vacation. On the evening of December 29th Jeanine got a message on her cell phone from Senator Buono's office apologizing for the short notice and explaining that the next morning Acting Governor Codey was going to sign Grace's Law. The governor wanted to know if Jeanine and her family would be available to join him for the ceremony.

Grace remembers, "We got a phone call telling us that they were going to pass Grace's Law. I remember my Mom was laughing and happy, and my Dad was, too. I was happier for Mom than I was for me."

"I clearly remember when we were in Florida when the law passed, and Governor Cody called my Mom. We were all really emotional. At first, it didn't sink in that - wow it actually happened! Things like that were real pinnacle moments," Shain said.

Jeanine was stunned. She could barely believe that after all these years it was becoming law - and that she would miss the signing! Even if they drove back then, they would not have made it on time. If she had known, she would have postponed her vacation. Through tears she immediately called her mother and father to tell them the news.

Another message was from Mary Katherine, one of Jeanine's biggest supporters and the mother of hearing-impaired twins, telling Jeanine that Senator Madden's office called to invite her and Summit Speech School's director Dr. Paskowitz to the signing.

Although ecstatic with the news of the passage, Mary Katherine felt as terrible as Jeanine that she wouldn't be there. Even though she wanted to go, Jeanine stressed that the most important thing was that it was being signed into law. She insisted that they be there even without her and her family.

Bill said, "Jeanine was on the phone with everybody. She was so disappointed and upset that she couldn't be there, but it was one of those things where if you didn't sign then, the legislature could turn over, and it could go right back to where it was before. We certainly didn't want that to happen after all Jeanine's years of hard work."

Jeanine believed it was important to have some of the people there who made it happen - especially children. She felt that although the law was named for Grace, it was not just Grace's Law. It was for all of New Jersey's deaf and hard of hearing children. Mary Katherine reluctantly agreed to appear on Jeanine's behalf, where she would be able to read a speech Jeanine had written.

"You cannot imagine how disappointed we are that we can't be there. For many years we have dreamed of this historical moment when Grace's Law would become a reality in New Jersey. Today is truly a great day for the children of New Jersey and their families. Our faith that the right things would be done never wavered, and we are forever indebted to Acting Governor Codey and New Jersey's legislators. Hopefully, other states will follow the leadership of New Jersey, and there will be national reform for hearing aid insurance legislation. Today our voices were heard and children have been given the priceless gift of sound and many doors have been opened for them. What a way to ring in the New Year! With deep gratitude and tears of joy."

Grace also wrote a note to be read by supporter Caitlyn D'Alessio while Kaitlyn Weatherby held up her picture, "Since Grace's Law has passed I would like to thank all the people who joined and helped us to pass Grace's Law. Grace's Law is very important to my family and me, and it is an honor to bear its name. With the help of everyone we have helped New Jersey's deaf and hard of hearing children to be able to hear. This is UNBELIEVABLE and REMARKABLE!"

JEANINE'S FINAL SAY

Finally, with a heavy heart I went to bed. And try as I might, that night sleep would not come as I tossed and turned through all of my emotions. I lay silently staring at the ceiling as tears of joy, and I don't know what, self-pity maybe, fell down my cheeks and the pillow muffled my cries. Nine years, four legislative sessions, almost 9,000 petition signatures, thousands of letters and phone calls, 57 sponsors and insurmountable odds - I just could not believe that after all that we weren't going to be there.

When we were all rising early the next morning on December 30, 2008 I had a meltdown while Grace was in the shower. Bill and the boys did their best to comfort me even though they were just as upset that we weren't going to be there.

I kept telling myself over and over again to accept it and revel in the fact that it was law. Fortunately, the enormity of the accomplishment was slowing sinking in. Finally, it reached a point when Grace without her hearing aids on and dripping wet in her towel stepped out of the bathroom, and I said to Bill and the boys I feel like Rocky when he beat Apollo Creed. Not caring who I woke up in the rooms next to us I yelled to Grace at the top of my lungs so she could hear, "Yo Grace! We did it!"

And with that I was back to banging away at the keyboard. The first new message in my inbox was from my brother Doug, and he wrote only one thing, which tugged at my heartstrings again. "No Jeanine...you did it! Congratulations!"

Then I wrote this to my parents and brothers. "I didn't sleep much last night. I think I am going through the five stages of death...first shock and now anger. This is like some cruel sick joke. After nine years of blood, sweat and tears and all the things I did to get this passed to not be there is killing me. What kept me always going was "someday you will be there when the Governor signs it into law." And then when I think of how many times I waited for legislators to respond or post it for a vote etc. etc. and they can't wait five days for us. I feel like I am not getting final closure since we aren't there for the final moment. It should be Grace standing there today. I don't even feel like celebrating."

After my family read that, I would be willing to bet my last penny that the phones were ringing off the hook. My brother Chris wrote to me "Congratulations and pop open a bottle of champagne! Let us know if you want us to represent you. I feel like it's the scene where the brother makes the surprise visit home from winning the Congressional Medal of Honor in It's a Wonderful Life."

It had never dawned on me that perhaps someone in my family could go. I quickly wrote him back explaining how much it would mean to us if he could go. Chris immediately wrote me saying he would be honored to accept on our behalf if I wanted him to. Knowing he would be there, a calm like I had never felt before washed over me. He quite literally dropped everything for me that day.

I will treasure the ensuing email messages flying back and forth between us all as the clock was ticking closer and closer to 10:30.

Chris had absolutely no clue what he was in for. I told him when you arrive tell them whatever you need to get in. Say you are Grace's Godfather! He called Governor Corzine's aide Terry West for the logistics since this was a first for all of us. He explained that he lived in Northern New Jersey but could be in Trenton in an hour or so. And boy was my friend and supporter Mary Katherine happy to see him walk through the door because he then read my speech so she didn't have to!

Not surprising our notable absence was not sitting well with Doug nor was he going to let it slide. When Terry West sent him and others a notice that morning about the signing, Doug reached out to Governor Corzine and Terry West on my behalf. He reiterated Grace and I were not available and told them flat out "I would hope, at the very least, after all their hard work, they will be given a signed copy of the bill as well as one of the executive pens used to sign it. Thank you for your cooperation."

An hour later we checked out of the hotel and headed over to the Gulf Coast. I received a short and simple text message from Chris "It's done," and a weight whose existence I had denied was once and for all lifted off my shoulders.

That afternoon my normally quiet cell phone was ringing off the hook. Even Acting Governor Codey personally called me because he, too, felt bad that we weren't there. I can't recall what I had for breakfast yesterday, but I can recall how surreal it felt to be walking along the shore of the Gulf Coast being interview by NPR radio!

The Star-Ledger finally ran the story on Grace that they had interviewed us for weeks earlier that very same day. It was a huge spread taking up most of the New Jersey section's front page with her picture and the headline, "She Made Lawmakers Listen." And it was all on the evening news!

It was killing us not to be able see or read these things at the time, but everyone bought us copies of all the papers that ran stories and made DVD recordings. But it was grateful messages over the subsequent weeks that meant the most to us,

"YOU changed my family to believe that if you lobby hard enough, people will care. YOU changed my children. They had a learning experience, which they will NEVER get from a book in school."

We rung in the New Year with hats, horns and fireworks on the beach, and we popped open quite a few bottles of champagne to celebrate our accomplishment! And on that January 1st as I wrote out New Year's resolutions for the first time in more years than I cared to remember it did not include "Pass Grace's Law."

SOMEBODY PINCH ME

Jeanine came home to a whirlwind of congratulatory wishes and press interviews. The first thing she did was write a long thank you to all of the supporters over the years. Acting Governor Codey did indeed mail Grace a package with a copy of the signed law and one of the pens he used to sign it.

After the signing on December 30th, they told Jeanine's brother Chris and Jeanine's supporters who had attended that upon the family's return Governor Corzine was going to arrange a special ceremonial signing of the law in his office.

On Friday, January 23rd shortly before 1:00 pm Jeanine's family and her mother arrived at the State Capitol. They were whisked into the Governor's inner office to meet him before the ceremony in his outer office. He had barely reached out his hand to Jeanine when the tears came down her face. "I can't explain it. I was swept away with emotion. It didn't matter if he was green, black or white or-Democratic or Republican. To have this man in such power greet and personally thank us for our efforts was too much."

Jeanine didn't know what to expect at a ceremonial signing, but she never expected the throngs of people, press, and fanfare. She also didn't expect both Governor Corzine and Senator Codey and others like Senator Turner to take time out of their busy schedules to honor them.

They went out of their way to make it a very momentous occasion even though it had already been a law for almost a month. Both Corzine and Codey signed yet another copy of the law flanked by many of the children and Grace – who was even given the honor of handing each child a pen.

Shain remembered that day; "I was young when it was all taking place. I remember it was pretty cool to be at the state capital meeting all these senators and assemblymen. Meeting people like Governor Corzine - I thought it was the coolest thing in the world. I could tell my friends, 'guess who just met my mom? The governor. For me it was awesome. At the same time, it was also a really good learning experience for me to be exposed to all that - especially at a young age. Most people don't have an understanding of local and state politics, and I think even for our family it was learning process with my mom trying to get the bill passed. I could see how much of a struggle it actually is to get legislation passed in the state."

Jeanine was glad Grace and she had prepared something to say because after the Governor spoke to the press it was their turn at the podium.

Grace remembers, "I had to give my speech. I remember meeting the Governor. I shook his hand, and he said we will go outside the room, so you guys can talk. We went outside, and I went on the podium to speak. It was a really small room, and people were talking. The lights were really bright, and people were videotaping me. I saw my family members in the back - my cousins, aunts, and uncles. After that I remember Governor Corzine walked me over to a table a few feet away from the podium. He signed the paper with like 17 different pens. He came over to me, and then I handed to them to the kids who were surrounding him when he signed it."

One of Jeanine's proudest moments was watching Grace on the news that night speaking eloquently and crystal clear, "Thank you Governor Corzine and Senator Codey for signing Grace's law in front of me and my friends and making it a law in New Jersey. When I turn on my hearing aids, it is a whole new world for me. Without them my world is blank. So many more children will be able to get hearing aids now and hear like me...."

"We felt famous with all of the cameras! Then reality set in that we were just ordinary people," said Luke.

"When we got the news that we would miss the signing, at first my Mom was in disbelief. Then it settled in and she started crying. I was also kind of mad because we couldn't be there. But we got to see Governor Corzine at the next one, and I remember feeling happy and joyful about it," Grace said. "I had to give a speech in front of the press and it made me realize that after all of the years and hard work it really paid off, and I wouldn't even be able to speak to them if I didn't have my hearing aids. Today I'm not afraid of public speaking because I've spoken so many times in front of so many people. I don't have a fear of presenting. I really know that it's important to stand up for what what's right."

Bill noted, "When our particular situation with Grace began, we started by feeling skeptical about whether Summit Speech School was going to be the answer or not. But, we learned with the right people helping and the technology available today, hope is not lost. If you look for it, there's almost always something out there that can improve or help or make the situation better than what it is. We dealt with adversity both with Grace being hearing impaired and Jeanine's fight for Grace's Law. They were two separate issues. One was looking out for the welfare and well being of our child. The other was looking at how the heck you can change something in this world. In either case, they certainly don't make it easy."

"Over the years, Grace has handled her hearing loss remarkably well. It is tough growing up for any kid. I think it's even tougher for them to grow up being different. They don't want to be looked at as the 'odd' person. They want to be like everybody else. Grace has adapted very well, and we couldn't be happier with the progress that she has made both academically and personally. I know it has been difficult for her at times. She does struggle to hear in certain environments, but we had a lot of good help along the way that made it easier for her."

"I'm able to accomplish many things with my hearing aids," Grace said, "starting with my learning to listen and speak. Now I can hear people and all sounds around me! There are so many things like cheerleading, gymnastics and dance classes where my hearing aids make a difference. I can enjoy music and sing. I also do really well in school with my hearing aids including making Principal Honor Roll in high school. I am able to hear people speak. I don't always ask 'What?' 'What did you say?' or ask them to yell or anything. It's a lot easier to communicate because I can participate in conversations with my family and friends. I probably wouldn't have many friends either, since I wouldn't be able to talk as well with them. My hearing aids have changed my life. Not being able to hear is a huge thing in your life because you will have trouble communicating with friends and family. That's why Grace's Law is important to my family and me. We know access to hearing aids can really change a person's life for the better."

"I think what we learned is that if you're really set on trying to change something, it can be changed," said Bill. "But you are going to need to be in it for the long haul and prepare yourself. Like anything else in this world, change doesn't happen easily. If you want something, you have to work for it - sometimes harder than you think. You might be discouraged, but you always have to keep fighting through that. I think this experience has definitely changed us. You can't imagine what life would have been like if it hadn't happened."

AN AFTERWORD FROM JEANINE

It was hard to believe that we had been fighting for this thing basically since Grace's birth. I honestly believe that God does work in strange ways and had the law passed when Grace was three it would not have been as meaningful and certainly would not have had such a positive impact on her life with regards to the lessons learned and her also contributing to the accomplishment and making a difference in the world.

She will always remember this along with the other children who made lawmakers listen and improved the lives of many.

Grace's Law was truly an example of grass roots lobbying and that perseverance and commitment pay-off. Passage of this law was necessary for New Jersey's deaf and hard of hearing children, which is why we never quit.

Society takes for granted our five senses until we don't have one. We literally were the voice for the voiceless because without hearing aids these children won't be able to hear and won't have a voice. Children should not be denied the opportunity to listen and speak. I know it has become a cliché, but no child should be left behind. They are our future, and we can expect great things from these kids.

Sometimes the little people, regardless of age, can get lost in big government and politics. I stand before you to tell you that your government can work for you. Citizens, even children, can take action, make a difference and most especially, right a wrong.

It's been said that actions speak louder than words. I believe in this case it was the actions of many - and more powerful - the words of these youngsters that made the difference. To quote Helen Keller, "Alone we can do so little. Together we can do so much."

Like in the visions of my dreams, Grace and I were standing next to the Governor looking out into the blinding lights as they were all there sharing the victory with us. I could see on the one side Bill, Shain, Luke and my mother. Way in the back I couldn't miss standing tall and proud my brothers Chris and Doug with their families. There also in front of me was even Carol Granaldi, AG Bell President Gary Kirsch, Pam Paskowitz, the employees of the Division of Deaf and Hard of Hearing. Not to mention the D'Alessio family and so many more! Only this time it wasn't just a dream. It was real.

We need to remember that Grace's Law is one small victory within a much bigger fight. The children of New Jersey may have won this round, but we need insurance companies to cover hearing aids, not just in New Jersey, but also across the country. Although there are some states trying to pass similar legislation, it is such a shame that every state individually has to struggle and go through all this to get hearing aid coverage.

Worse still even in New Jersey and every state there will always exist a population of children who can't benefit from these state mandates as a result of employers with self-funded plans as they are protected federally under ERISA. As a result of the EEOC dropping the case, my ex-employer never changed their health plan to cover hearing aids and is also exempt from Grace's Law.

Furthermore, except for about two states, coverage is only extended to children. Hearing loss is a lifelong problem, and these children with hearing loss will continue to need hearing aids into adulthood.

They should not be forgotten just because they grow up. We don't live in Peter Pan's world. We do grow old. Nor should adults be punished because they either can't afford an insurance plan that covers hearing aids, or their employer refuses to pay for it, since health plans that include hearing aid coverage are usually more expensive. It should be a standard inclusive benefit no matter what the plan for everyone.

This is a national problem, not just a problem for children or the elderly, but also a problem for everyone who needs hearing aids and their families. And the problem is only going to get worse as a result of those losing their hearing due to overexposure from loud noise such as through headphones or all of the soldiers returning home from war with hearing loss from wounds. We need Federal "hearing" insurance reform NOW.

THANK YOU FROM JEANINE

"Thank you, Governor Corzine and his aide Terry West and Acting Governor Codey for recognizing our efforts and making Grace's Law a reality in New Jersey. We greatly appreciate this honor of witnessing the law being signed again.

Thank you to the Primary Sponsors Senator Buono, Senator Lance, Assemblyman Roberts and Assemblyman Conaway for their unwavering support over the years. We had 57 sponsors for this legislation and we are grateful to all of them.

I know Governor Corzine and Acting Governor Codey already recognized key organizations like the NJ Division of Deaf and Hard of Hearing that always supported this legislation. However, I'd like to add to that list the following: New Jersey's Alexander Graham Bell Association; New Jersey's Hearing Loss Association of America; New Jersey's American Speech/Language and Hearing Association, the Better Hearing Institute and the Hearing Access organization. Since the original signing I have expressed my gratitude to all those involved in New Jersey's hearing aid insurance legislation including our family. It was a collective effort that I hope all involved feel a sense of pride knowing that they helped make this law a reality in New Jersey."

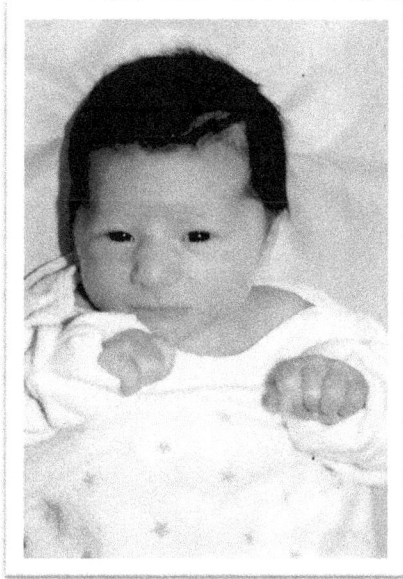

Grace, newborn, in
St. Clare's Hospital
Denville, NJ

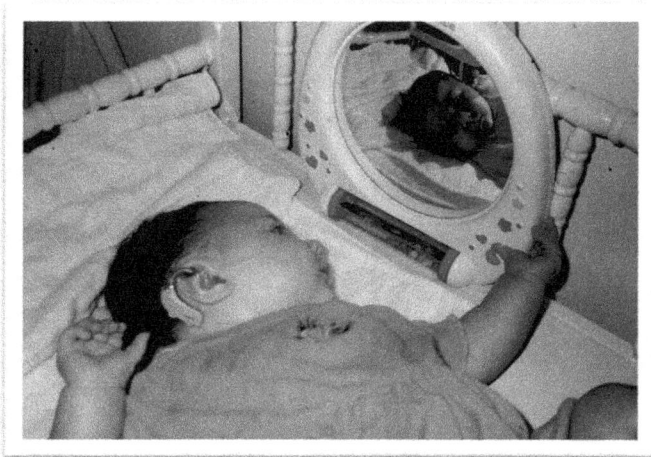

Grace, age 3 months, with first pair of hearing aids

Grace, age 3, with Senator Anthony Bucco

Grace, age 3, in make-up and wardrobe for Toys R Us ad

Grace, age 5, graduating from the Summit Speech School

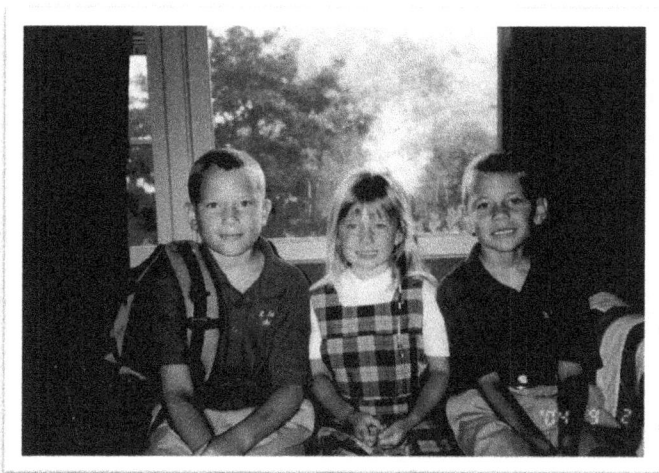

Grace, age 5, first day of school starting mainstream Kindergarten at St. Mary's School – Getting ready for bus with brothers Shain and Luke

Grace, age 5, with Senator Joseph Vitale

Jeanine, in 2004, with Miss America Heather Whitestone

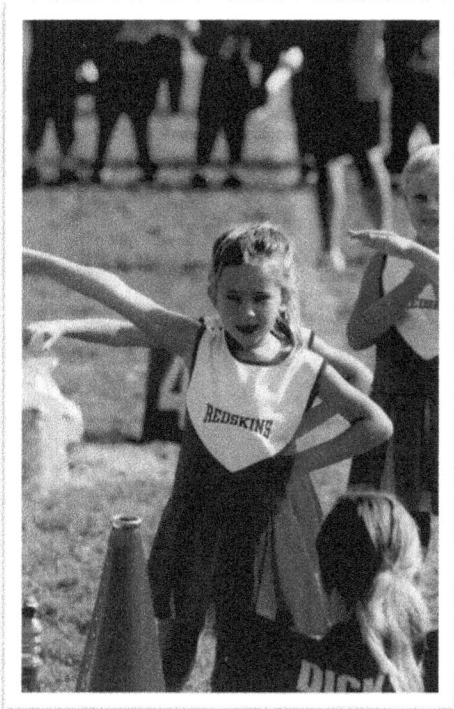

Grace first year cheering age 6

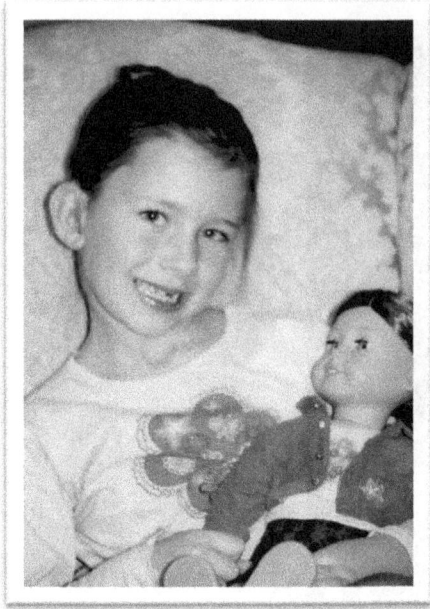

Grace with her American Girl doll

Grace, age 9, with Senator Barbara Buono and other children with hearing loss

Grace's Law 2008 Walk4HearingTeam

Grace, age 9, at Assembly House vote with Speaker
of the House Assemblyman Joseph Roberts and
Assemblywoman Marcia Karrow

Grace and family celebrating in Florida after law
signed December 2018

Grace's Godfather, Chris Williamson, speaking on
their behalf at Acting Governor Codey's signing of
Grace's Law in December 2008

Grace's family with Governor Corzine in his office in
Trenton, NJ 2009

Grace, age 9, meeting Governor Jon Corzine at Ceremonial
Signing at State Capitol in Trenton, NJ

www.ingramcontent.com/pod-product-compliance
Lightning Source LLC
LaVergne TN
LVHW011230080426
835509LV00005B/413